Holy Hiatus

ritual and community in public art

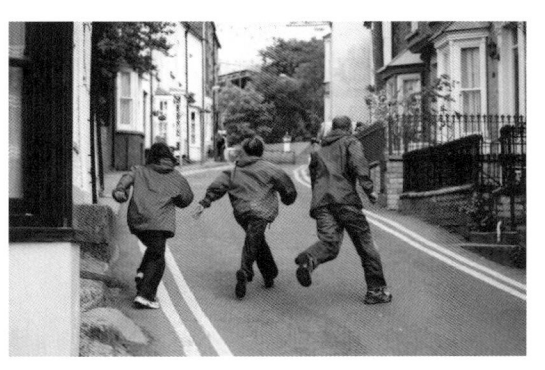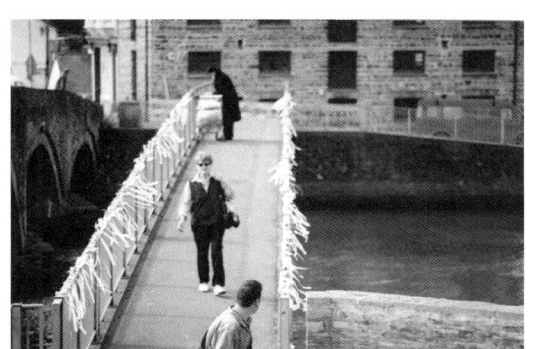

Holy Hiatus

ritual and community in public art

edited by Ruth Jones

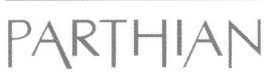

Parthian
The Old Surgery
Napier Street
Cardigan
SA43 1ED

www.parthianbooks.com

www.holyhiatus.co.uk

First published in 2010
© the contributors
All Rights Reserved

Edited by Ruth Jones

Translation by Ceri Jones

ISBN 978-1-905762-55-2

Cover images by Noëlle Pollington
Design & typesetting by Lucy Llewellyn
Printed and bound by

Published with the financial support of the Welsh Books Council

British Library Cataloguing in Publication Data

A cataloguing record for this book is available from the British Library

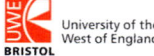 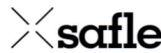 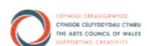 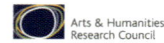 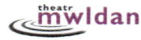 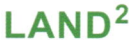 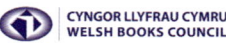

Contents

Ruth Jones

Ask anyone and you'll be assured, 'Sure, ritual has its place'. Like a dutiful servant, it should know that place and stay there. It ought not to be springing up underfoot, as if its place were everywhere.[1]

Experiments with Living Rituals

In May 2008, five temporary art events took place in public spaces in Cardigan as part of the project *Holy Hiatus*. Some people locally and from further afield knew about the events through publicity material or word of mouth, and made an active decision to attend, while others came across interventions unexpectedly whilst going about their daily business. A few people living in and around Cardigan became collaborators through their involvement in the artists' projects. The temporary, mobile and in some cases understated nature of the works meant that the impact was often subtle, but the artworks nonetheless created a ripple of effect for both active and incidental audiences, leading witnesses to wonder what they had just seen and to what extent they had knowingly, or unknowingly, participated in it.

In meditation and spiritual practices that involve ritual pattern making, 'holy hiatus' refers to the crossing of the boundary between inner and outer consciousness. The purpose of such practices is to allow inner processes to manifest as outer design or forms – a method that has strong analogies with art-making. *Holy Hiatus* focused on social ritual, community and public places to explore threshold, or 'liminal', states and examine the ways that artists can draw audiences into different, often unexpected, experiences of place through ritual. Liminal was originally an anthropological term referring to the central aspect of any ritual during which participants may have a transformative experience and is associated with both positive change and uncertainty. More recently, the word liminal has

Arbrofi gyda Defodau Byw

Ym mis Mai 2008, cynhaliwyd pum digwyddiad celfyddydol dros dro mewn mannau cyhoeddus yn Aberteifi fel rhan o'r prosiect *Holy Hiatus*. Yr oedd rhai pobl leol ac eraill yn gwybod am y digwyddiadau hyn drwy ddeunydd cyhoeddusrwydd neu wedi clywed sôn amdanynt, ac wedi penderfynu mynd i'w gweld, ac roedd eraill wedi taro ar y digwyddiadau ar hap. Daeth rhai pobl, a oedd yn byw yn Aberteifi a'r cylch, i gydweithio ar brosiectau'r artistiaid. Gan fod y gweithiau'n rhai dros dro, symudol a chynnil weithiau, cynnil hefyd oedd eu heffaith yn aml. Serch hynny, llwyddodd y gweithiau celf i blannu hedyn ym meddyliau'r gynulleidfa, y rhai a'u gwelodd yn unswydd neu ar hap, gan wneud iddynt feddwl am yr hyn a welsant ac i ba raddau yr oeddynt wedi cymryd rhan, boed o fwriad neu'n ddiarwybod iddynt.

Mewn arferion myfyriol ac ysbrydol sydd yn ymwneud â chreu patrymau defodol, mae 'holy hiatus' yn cyfeirio at groesi'r ffin rhwng yr ymwybod mewnol ac allanol. Pwrpas ymarferion o'r fath yw caniatáu i'r prosesau mewnol eu hamlygu eu hunain yn gynllun neu ffurfiau allanol – yn debyg iawn i greu celfyddyd. Yr oedd *Holy Hiatus* yn canolbwyntio ar ddefodau cymdeithasol, cymunedau a mannau cyhoeddus er mwyn archwilio'r cyflwr trothwyol (sef profiadau sydd rhwng dau le) a gweld sut y gall artistiaid dynnu cynulleidfaoedd i mewn i brofiadau gwahanol o le drwy ddefod, a hynny'n aml yn annisgwyl. Term anthropolegol yn wreiddiol yw 'trothwyol' (*liminal*); mae'n cyfeirio at agwedd ganologol unrhyw ddefod y gallai pobl gael profiad trawsffurfiol drwyddi ac fe'i entered into cultural thinking in a number of different disciplines, particularly theatre and performance, but it can refer to any experience during which the normal linear and day-to-day experience of time and space is suspended and a different state of consciousness is achieved. 'Ritual' often conjures images of traditional religion or social occasions that reconfirm traditional authority, and while ritual can be conservative, this project hopes to demonstrate that ritual acts can also be creative and dynamic, having the capacity to introduce innovative understandings of identity, on both a personal and a social level, and to re-present places, often familiar ones, in new and invigorating ways.

Cardigan has been undergoing a process of regeneration for a number of years. In 2004 Theatr Mwldan reopened its doors in a purpose built new building, and helped to establish Cardigan as a focus in West Wales for art, theatre, world music and cinema. Following many years of involvement with community arts, the Small World Theatre raised funds for its own innovatively designed building, which was completed and opened to the public in 2008, Maura Hazelden's project for *Holy Hiatus* was the first event to take place in this space. Public opinion has been voracious, and often polarised over plans to regenerate Cardigan Castle grounds and house as a heritage site, and over the proposed semi-permanent public sculptural installation by Rafael Lozano-Hemmer in the River Teifi, supported by Channel 4's Big Art Project. It is not surprising, given the level of cultural activity taking place in this small town over the last few years, that its residents feel uncertain about its future. *Holy Hiatus* was an opportunity to explore this in-between or 'liminal' state of the town through a series of non-permanent, low-budget and place-sensitive events that attempted to bridge social and political differences through ritual activity that negotiates the space between tradition and innovation, between the past and the future, between

cysylltir â newid cadarnhaol ac ansicrwydd fel ei gilydd. Yn fwy diweddar, mae'r gair trothwyol wedi treiddio i'r meddylfryd diwylliannol mewn nifer o ddisgyblaethau gwahanol, yn arbennig theatr a pherfformio, ond gall gyfeirio at unrhyw brofiad pan fydd profiadau arferol a phrofiadau o dydd i ddydd o amser a gofod yn peidio, a cheir math gwahanol o ymwybod. Yn aml mae 'defod' yn awgrymu crefydd draddodiadol neu achlysuron cymdeithasol sydd yn cadarnhau awdurdod traddodiadol. Ond er y gall y ddefod fod yn geidwadol, mae'r prosiect hwn yn gobeithio dangos y gall gweithredoedd defodol hefyd fod yn greadigol a deinamig, ac y gallant ennyn dealltwriaeth flaengar o hunaniaeth, ar lefel bersonol a chymdeithasol, a chyflwyno lleoedd o'r newydd, rhai cyfarwydd yn aml, mewn ffyrdd newydd a chyffrous.

Mae tref Aberteifi yn destun gwaith adfywio ers nifer o flynyddoedd. Yn 2004 ailagorodd Theatr Mwldan ei drysau mewn adeilad newydd pwrpasol a bu hyn o gymorth i greu enw i Aberteifi fel canolfan yng Ngorllewin Cymru ar gyfer celf, theatr, cerddoriaeth y byd a sinema. Ar ôl blynyddoedd o ymwneud â'r celfyddydau cymunedol, cododd Theatr Byd Bychan arian i godi ei adeilad blaengar ei hun, a chwblhawyd ac agorwyd yr adeilad i'r cyhoedd yn 2008. Prosiect Maura Hazelden i *Holy Hiatus* oedd y digwyddiad cyntaf i'w gynnal yn yr adeilad hwn. Mae'r farn gyhoeddus wedi bod yn llafar iawn, a bu cryn wahaniaeth barn ynglŷn â'r cynlluniau i adfywio gerddi a thŷ Castell Aberteifi yn safle treftadaeth, ac ynghylch gosodwaith cerfluniol cyhoeddus lled-barhaol arfaethedig gan Rafael Lozano-Hemmer yn afon Teifi gyda chefnogaeth *Big Art Project Channel 4*. Does ryfedd felly, o ystyried yr holl weithgarwch diwylliannol a fu'n digwydd yn y dref fach hon yn ystod y blynyddoedd diwethaf, fod ei thrigolion yn teimlo'n ansicr am ei dyfodol. Yr oedd *Holy Hiatus* yn gyfle i archwilio cyflwr trothwyol y dref drwy gyfres o ddigwyddiadau dros dro, ar

permanence and mutability, and between selfhood and community.

The project also sought to address how public art and site-specific works can function in a rural environment. There is a tendency to believe that a number of factors work against the success of rural experimental projects like this, such as the problem of locating sufficient funding sources, and bringing together an audience that is geographically scattered. Precedents existed in rural Wales, such as *Strata*, an international site-responsive project curated by Ann Mulrooney and Tim Davies in Strata Florida Abbey in 2005, and the artists' collective *ointment* have carried out live and site-specific projects in Ceredigion and Pembrokeshire since 2001, suggesting that innovative public art projects can reach local audiences. In addition, visitors will travel from cities or other rural places to attend these projects, demonstrating their contemporary relevance. *Holy Hiatus* focused on two inter-related possibilities: firstly, how to develop a better understanding of the relationships between art and ritual; secondly, can art that employs ritual contribute to a sense of community? Integral to these questions is the location of the project in a rural place where there is a complex relationship between traditional practices that retain elements of ritual (for example, farming and traditional religions) and contemporary lifestyles.

It is important to ask, what is meant when we talk about 'community' in relation to public art practice? Community is often referred to in the abstract as a place or group of people, whose existence is taken for granted but not examined closely, or alternatively as something lost from the past, to be mourned, which can never be recovered. *Holy Hiatus* drew on Grant Kester's approach to community and public art outlined in his book *Conversation Pieces*, in which he promotes the facilitation of dialogue and exchange through a process that can 'help us speak and

gyllideb fach, a fyddai'n gweddu i'w lleoliadau, ac a oedd yn ceisio pontio'r gwahaniaethau gwleidyddol a chymdeithasol drwy weithredu defodol sydd yn troedio'r gagendor rhwng y traddodiadol a'r newydd, rhwng y gorffennol a'r dyfodol, y parhaol a'r cyfnewidiol, a rhwng yr hunan a'r gymuned.

Yr oedd y prosiect hefyd yn ceisio ystyried sut y gall celf gyhoeddus a gweithiau'n ymwneud â lleoliadau penodol weithredu mewn amgylchedd gwledig. Mae tueddiad i gredu bod nifer o ffactorau'n gweithio yn erbyn llwyddiant prosiectau arbrofol gwledig fel hyn, megis problem dod o hyd i ffynonellau ariannol digonol, a dwyn ynghyd gynulleidfa sydd yn wasgaredig yn ddaearyddol. Yr oedd cynseiliau yn y Gymru wledig, er enghraifft *Strata*, prosiect rhyngwladol a oedd yn ymateb i'w safle, dan guraduriaeth Ann Mulrooney a Tim Davies, yn Abaty Ystrad Fflur yn 2005, a'r grŵp cydweithredol o artistiaid, *ointment*, sydd wedi bod yn cynnal prosiectau byw'n ymwneud â lleoliadau penodol yng Ngheredigion a sir Benfro er 2001. Awgryma hyn y gall prosiectau celf gyhoeddus blaengar gyrraedd cynulleidfaoedd lleol. Yn ogystal, bydd ymwelwyr yn teithio o ddinasoedd a mannau gwledig eraill i fynychu'r prosiectau hyn, ac mae hynny'n dangos eu bod yn berthnasol yn yr oes sydd ohoni. Mae *Holy Hiatus* yn canolbwyntio ar ddau bosibilrwydd cydberthnasol: yn gyntaf, sut i ddatblygu gwell dealltwriaeth o'r berthynas rhwng celf a defod; yn ail, a all celf sydd yn defnyddio defodau gyfrannu at ymdeimlad o gymuned? Yn greiddiol i'r cwestiynau hyn mae lleoliad y prosiect mewn ardal wledig lle mae perthynas gymhleth rhwng arferion traddodiadol sydd wedi cadw elfennau o ddefod (er enghraifft, ffermio a chrefyddau traddodiadol) a ffyrdd mwy cyfoes o fyw.

Mae'n bwysig gofyn beth a olygir wrth inni sôn am 'gymuned' yng nghyd-destun celf gyhoeddus? Cyfeirir at gymuned yn aml mewn ffordd haniaethol fel lle neu grŵp o bobl, y cymerir eu

imagine beyond the limits of fixed identities, official discourse, and the perceived inevitability of partisan political conflict'. He calls this process 'dialogical', and projects that adopt this approach 'unfold through a process of performative interaction'.[2]

Holy Hiatus could be seen as an experiment in 'performative interaction' and this publication aims to extend this dialogue beyond the actual artworks, which have left no physical trace, but exist in people's memories and as documentation in the form of images and sound, and in recorded audience responses to the works. The book also offers a contextual framework for the project within a field of cultural theory that ranges from contemporary art to anthropology, sociology and religious studies. There are four essays included in the publication: Bobby Alexander's essay has been adapted from his paper from the *Holy Hiatus* symposium and provides the social and anthropological context for the project, defining liminality and demonstrating how anthropologist Victor Turner's theories can be useful for art practices that employ ritual. My own essay draws on a series of interviews with audience members, who witnessed first hand the artworks for *Holy Hiatus*. The essay presents the differing, sometimes diametrical, readings of the artworks in relation to people's perceptions of ritual. The communal and participatory aspects of ritual are explored as well as the possibilities for achieving an altered state of mind during ritual action.

Samantha Hurn's contribution is based on a transcript of the conversation between Hurn and Anna Lucas during the symposium. Hurn introduces us to anthropological understandings of the complex social rituals surrounding our relationships with domesticated and wild animals, particularly in West Wales, and places these in context with Lucas's previous film works that explore human – animal relationships and her new film *Begail Foxwell Whip* created for *Holy Hiatus*. Iain Biggs's essay is in two parts: the first half is an academic

bodolaeth yn ganiataol ond heb ei harchwilio'n fanwl, neu fel arall fel rhywbeth a gollwyd o'r gorffennol, i alaru amdano oherwydd na ddaw fyth yn ei ôl. Yr oedd *Holy Hiatus* yn tynnu ar agwedd Grant Kester at gelf gymunedol a chyhoeddus a amlinellir yn ei lyfr *Conversation Pieces*. Yn y gyfrol hon mae'n annog hyrwyddo deialog a chyfnewid syniadau drwy broses sydd yn gallu 'ein helpu i siarad a dychmygu y tu hwnt i ffiniau hunaniaethau sefydlog, disgwrs swyddogol a'r dybiaeth fod gwrthdaro gwleidyddol pleidiol yn anorfod'. Mae'n galw'r broses hon yn 'ddeialogaidd' ac mae prosiectau sydd yn arddel yr agwedd hon yn 'datblygu drwy broses o ryngweithio perfformiadol'.

Gellid gweld *Holy Hiatus* fel arbrawf mewn 'rhyngweithio perfformiadol' a bwriad y cyhoeddiad hwn yw estyn y ddeialog hon y tu hwnt i'r gwaith celf ei hunan, nad yw wedi gadael unrhyw olion parhaol, ond sydd yn bodoli yng nghof pobl ac ar ffurf delweddau a sain, ac yn yr ymateb gan y gynulleidfa, a gafodd ei recordio. Mae'r llyfr hefyd yn rhoi'r prosiect yn ei gyd-destun ym maes damcaniaeth ddiwylliannol sy'n amrywio o gelf gyfoes i anthropoleg, cymdeithaseg ac astudiaethau crefyddol. Mae pedair erthygl yn y cyhoeddiad: mae erthygl Bobby Alexander wedi ei haddasu o'i bapur yn symposiwm *Holy Hiatus* ac yn darparu'r cyd-destun cymdeithasol ac anthropolegol ar gyfer y prosiect, gan ddiffinio'r trothwyol a dangos sut y gall damcaniaethau'r anthropolegydd Victor Turner fod yn ddefnyddiol o ran celfyddyd sydd yn defnyddio defodau. Mae fy erthygl innau'n tynnu ar gyfres o gyfweliadau ag aelodau o'r gynulleidfa a welodd drostynt eu hunain waith celf *Holy Hiatus*. Mae'r erthygl yn cyflwyno'r dehongliadau gwahanol, cyferbyniol weithiau, o'r gwaith celf o ran sut mae pobl yn gweld defodau. Mae agweddau cymunedol a chyfranogol ar y ddefod yn cael eu harchwilio yn ogystal â'r posibiliadau o ran newid cyflwr y meddwl yn ystod gweithgareddau defodol.

discussion, the second a loosely woven presentation of song lyric fragments and images relating to the England/Scotland Borders ballads. Together they suggest that greater attention to singing or hearing old quasi-pagan songs, perhaps almost as an everyday type of ritual, may help us better understand our communal place.

Interspersed between the texts are documentary images and texts relating to the five new artworks created for *Holy Hiatus*. The artists who were invited to participate in *Holy Hiatus* all have a history of responding sensitively to the sites in which they find themselves working. Their projects operated at many nuanced levels and were interpreted in varied ways by audiences, as will become clear throughout this publication, so a brief description will suffice here. Alastair MacLennan worked on the footbridge over the River Teifi for twelve hours, tying ribbon, greenery and paper boats to the railings and talking to curious users of the bridge. Simon Whitehead worked with dancers Kate Willis and Andrea Buckley to create an improvised dance, *Drift*, through the town over three days that followed the flow of the tides. Yvonne Buchheim created a public performance at Cardigan Swimming Pool in collaboration with two local swimmers and two singers. Maura Hazelden collaborated with acoustic singer Lou Laurens and created a six-hour performance in the Small World Theatre that explored ritual and prayer through repetitive movement. Anna Lucas spent three weeks meeting teenagers in West Wales who were actively involved with working animals, in order to gather film footage for a new video installation, *Begail Foxwell Whip*, that was exhibited in the Pendre Art Gallery.

A year on, *Holy Hiatus* has spontaneously developed a life of its own, with two of the artists' projects extending beyond the initial events. In conjunction with Safle, Buchheim's performance in the swimming pool has led to an eight-week public audio installation during April and May 2009 titled *Earworms* in which swimmers

Mae cyfraniad Samantha Hurn yn seiliedig ar drawsgrifiad o'r drafodaeth rhwng Hurn ac Anna Lucas yn ystod y symposiwm. Mae Hurn yn cyflwyno dealltwriaeth anthropolegol o'r defodau cymdeithasol cymhleth sy'n rhan annatod o'n perthynas ag anifeiliaid dof a gwyllt, yn enwedig yng Ngorllewin Cymru, ac yn rhoi hyn yng nghyd-destun gwaith ffilm blaenorol Lucas sydd yn archwilio'r berthynas rhwng bodau dynol ac anifeiliaid a'i ffilm newydd, *Begail Foxwell Whip*, a grëwyd ar gyfer *Holy Hiatus*. Mae erthygl Iain Biggs mewn dwy ran; yn y rhan gyntaf ceir trafodaeth academaidd, ac yn yr ail ran ceir plethwaith llac o eiriau caneuon a delweddau o faledi gororau'r Alban a Lloegr. Gyda'i gilydd maent yn awgrymu y gallwn, drwy roi rhagor o sylw i ganu neu wrando ar hen ganeuon lled-baganaidd, bron fel rhyw fath o ddefod ddyddiol, efallai, ddeall yn well ein lle yn y gymuned.

Yma a thraw yn y testun mae delweddau dogfennol a thestunau sydd yn ymwneud â'r pum gwaith celf newydd a grëwyd ar gyfer *Holy Hiatus*. Mae gan yr artistiaid a wahoddwyd i gymryd rhan yn *Holy Hiatus* hanes o ymateb yn sensitif i'r mannau lle maent yn gweithio. Roedd sawl haen i'w prosiectau a chawsant eu dehongli mewn sawl ffordd gan gynulleidfaoedd. Fe ddaw hynny'n glir yn y cyhoeddiad hwn, felly bydd disgrifiad byr yn ddigonol yma. Bu Alastair MacLennan yn gweithio ar bont droed dros afon Teifi am ddeuddeg awr, gan glymu rhubanau, deiliach a chychod papur i'r rheiliau a siarad â defnyddwyr chwilfrydig y bont. Bu Simon Whitehead yn gweithio gyda'r dawnswyr Kate Willis ac Andrea Buckley i greu dawns fyrfyfyr, *Drift*, a aeth drwy'r dref dros dridiau yn dilyn llif y llanw. Crëodd Yvonne Buchheim berfformiad cyhoeddus ym Mhwll Nofio Aberteifi ar y cyd â dau nofiwr lleol a dau ganwr. Bu Maura Hazelden yn cydweithio â'r gantores acwstig Lou Laurens i lunio perfformiad chwe awr yn Theatr Byd Bychan a oedd yn archwilio defod a gweddi drwy ailadrodd symudiadau.

could hear snippets of audio recordings from her *Song Archive* transmitted through underwater speakers. Hazelden and Laurens have extended their collaborative venture by re-creating their performance using recordings from the original event and new live elements in the Small World Theatre on the same date in 2009 and in years to come. This unprompted evolution is what makes temporary public art so exciting and demonstrates that rituals are always being reinvented to reflect contemporary lived experience.

Treuliodd Anna Lucas dair wythnos yn cwrdd â phobl ifanc yn eu harddegau yng Ngorllewin Cymru a oedd yn gweithio gydag anifeiliaid gwaith, er mwyn casglu deunydd ffilm ar gyfer gosodiad fideo newydd, *Begail Foxwell Whip*, a gafodd ei ddangos yn Oriel Gelf Pendre.

Flwyddyn yn ddiweddarach, mae *Holy Hiatus* wedi datblygu ohono'i hun, gyda dau o brosiectau'r artistiaid yn parhau wedi i'r prosiect ddod i ben. Ar y cyd â Safle, arweiniodd perfformiad Buchheim yn y pwll nofio at waith sain cyhoeddus am wyth wythnos yn ystod misoedd Ebrill a Mai 2009 o'r enw *Earworms*, lle gallai nofwyr glywed darnau o recordiadau sain o'i *Song Archive* a ddarlledwyd drwy seinyddion o dan y dŵr. Mae Hazelden a Laurens wedi estyn eu menter gydweithredol drwy ail-greu eu perfformiad gan ddefnyddio recordiadau o'r digwyddiad gwreiddiol ac elfennau newydd byw yn Theatr Byd Bychan ar yr un dyddiad yn 2009 ac yn y blynyddoedd i ddod. Yr esblygiad digymell hwn yw'r hyn sydd yn gwneud celf gyhoeddus dros dro mor gyffrous ac mae'n dangos bod defodau'n cael eu dyfeisio o'r newydd o hyd i adlewyrchu profiadau'r bywyd cyfoes

Holy Hiatus

ritual and community in public art

Alastair MacLennan

Lure in Rule

Actuation on footbridge over the River Teifi, Cardigan
5 a.m. – 5 p.m. Friday 23rd May 2008

Actuation comes from the verb to actuate, which means to communicate motion to, to cause the operation of, to cause to do, to function. It is related to the word actual, which means existing in fact; real (as distinct from ideal), existing now, current. Emphasis is on what is real in the present moment. Actuating interfuses performing with installing.

Alastair MacLennan

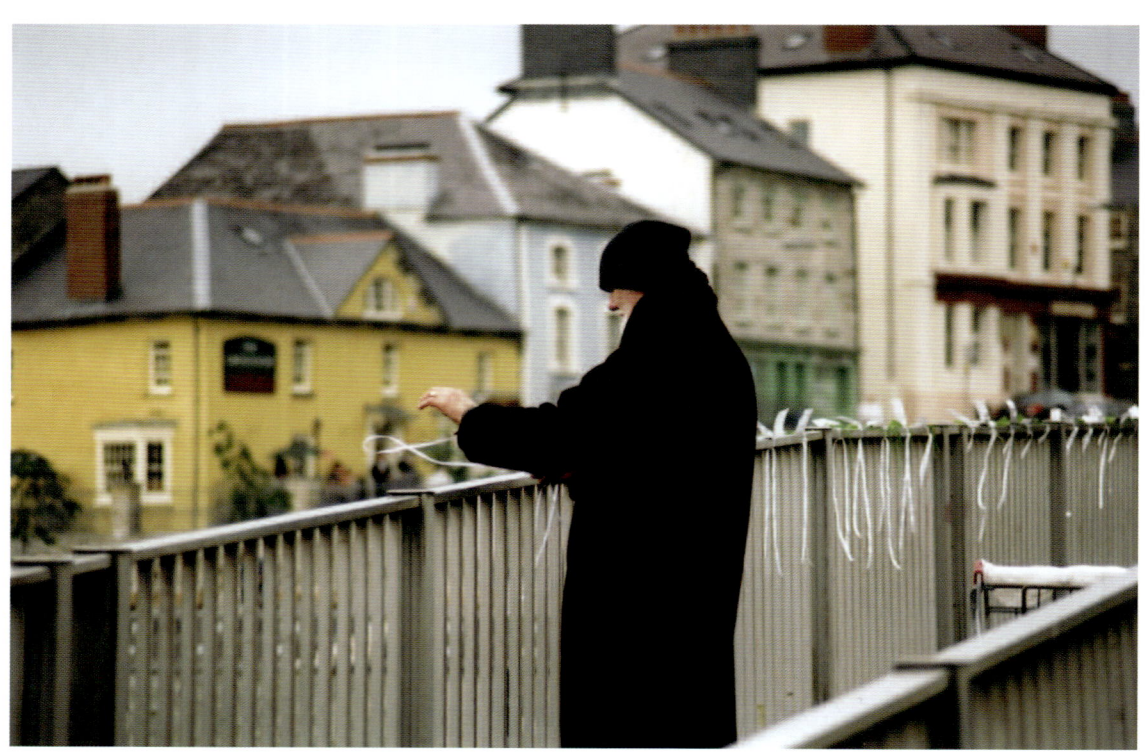

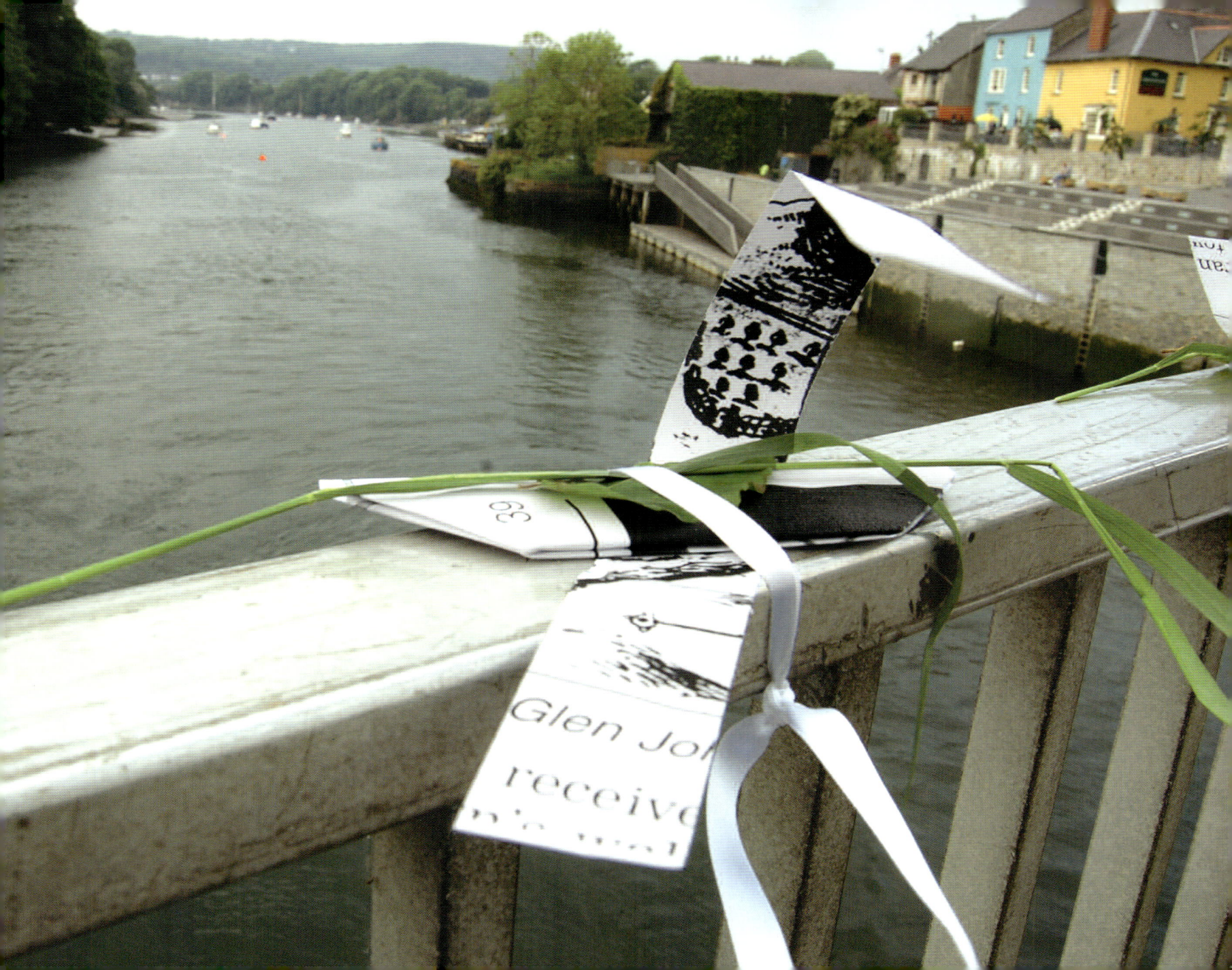

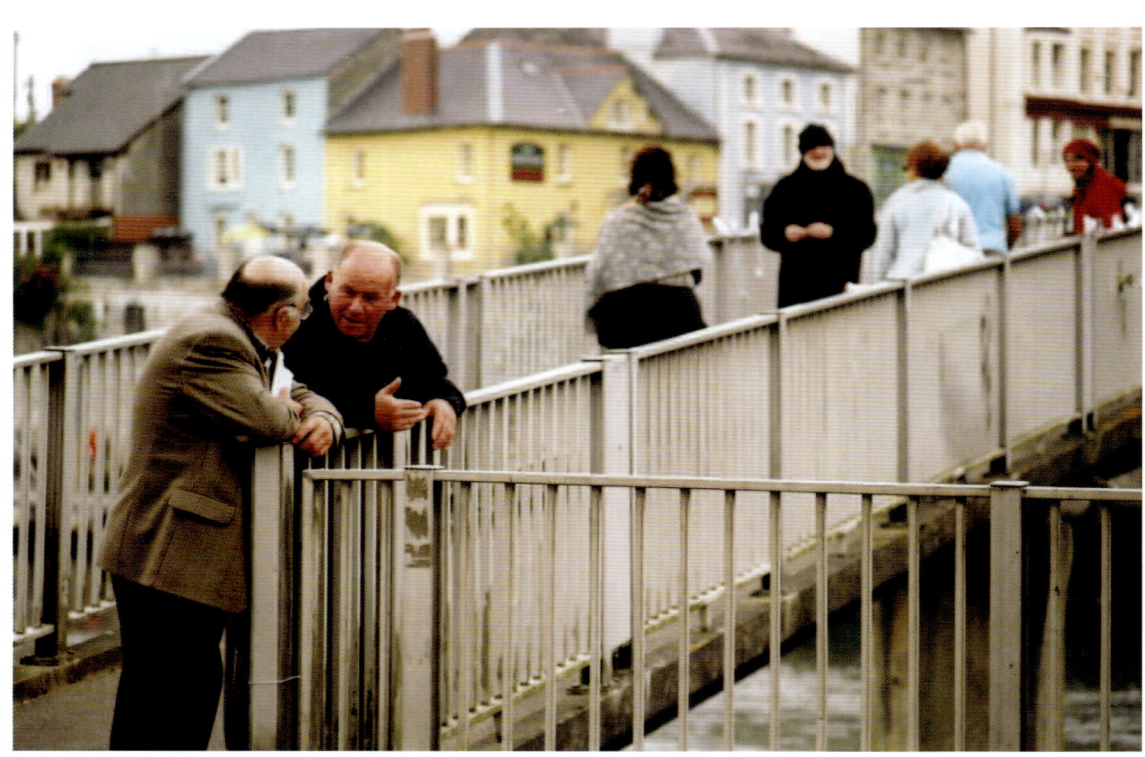

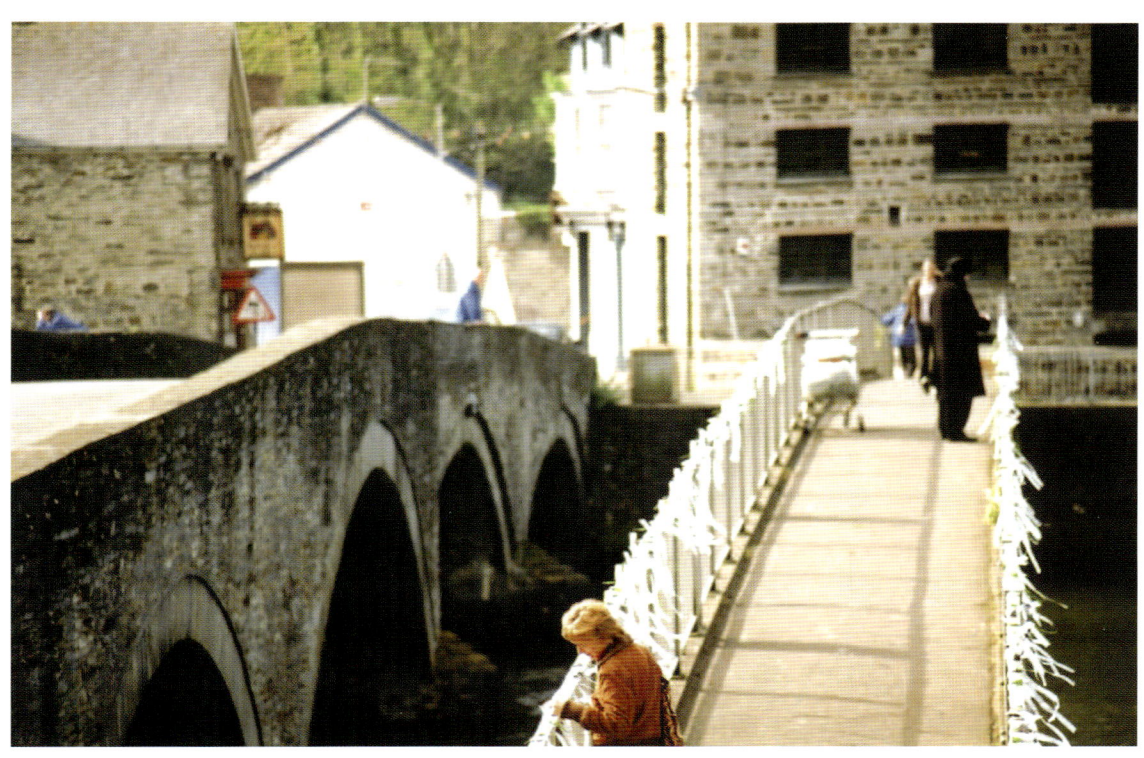

'Hi,' he said, looking up at me with clear blue eyes full of presence and yet deep with a sense of emptiness and space. There was no shift in the body language, no change of character, no returning from another place, he just kept on rhythmicaly layering and knotting. His eyes mirrored for me something sacred, profound, real. He was compeletely present and included me in that presence, meeting me with dignity in that moment. I had been on the outside observing but now I was woven into his ritual, now inside, part of source, not effect. I stuttered out 'Hi' softly back as this act of exchange drew me in into a transformative place and drew a smile from my very inner core. A shift in consciousness. A meeting on a bridge in Cardigan, Wales. Friday 30th March. A partaking in a creative ritual, an 'actuation' by artist Alastair MacLennan entitled *Lure in Rule.*

The journey to this bridge began in the West of Ireland, where two fellow performance artists and I left in search of the promise of ritual art to be experienced in the streets of Cardigan. Expectation was around every street corner. Finally we observed Alastair MacLennan from a distance, a figure dressed in a long black wool coat and cap, moving slowly on a foot bridge with a shopping trolley beside him.

By choosing a narrow foot bridge adjacent to the Old Town Bridge, across the River Teifi, and being there from 5 a.m. to 5 p.m., MacLennan took over a space ripe with potential for exchange and intersection with the public. Crossing of the bridge required passers to walk by him, often very close to him, and to step around the shopping tolley that held the elements included in the ritual. This bridge, a liminal space in itself, over moving water, became a very contained vessel with very clear boundaries to hold the ritual and involve the public.

Stepping onto the bridge I was quickly drawn into the movement of MacLennan's hands that were the focus of attention in his darkly covered body. With the clarity of an alchemist, his hands slowly and sequentially took from the shopping trolley where they were stacked in neat piles folded A4 sheets of black and white photocopied text and image, previously made paper boats and large green leaves. He layered the elements on top of each other, placed them on the handrail of the footbridge and tied them together with long green strips of grass. Then at the same point longer strips of white ribbon were tied on. Interweaving the elements and through exact repetition gradually over twelve hours every single metal join of the parallel with the perpendicular on the bridge had its own serene 'bunting'.

MacLennan's choreographed movement, emerging from an embodied source, created a very interesting rhythm. The sequential pattern in the figure of eight, infinity, was revealed through doing the task: moving from one side of the bridge to the other, pausing to collect the material elements to be attached, pausing to tie and knot, returning to the trolley and repeating. This slow rhythm left the space for enveloping the audience in his ritual as he met my presence as I passed by. What emerged was a shift in consciousness. This is a beautiful and rare experience.

Later that day I returned to the bridge. People were interacting with the art work, touching, reading, pretending to ignore. In the wind the bundled ribbons moved with gentle dignity, the remains of an art memorial to some past reality.

Maria Kerin 2009

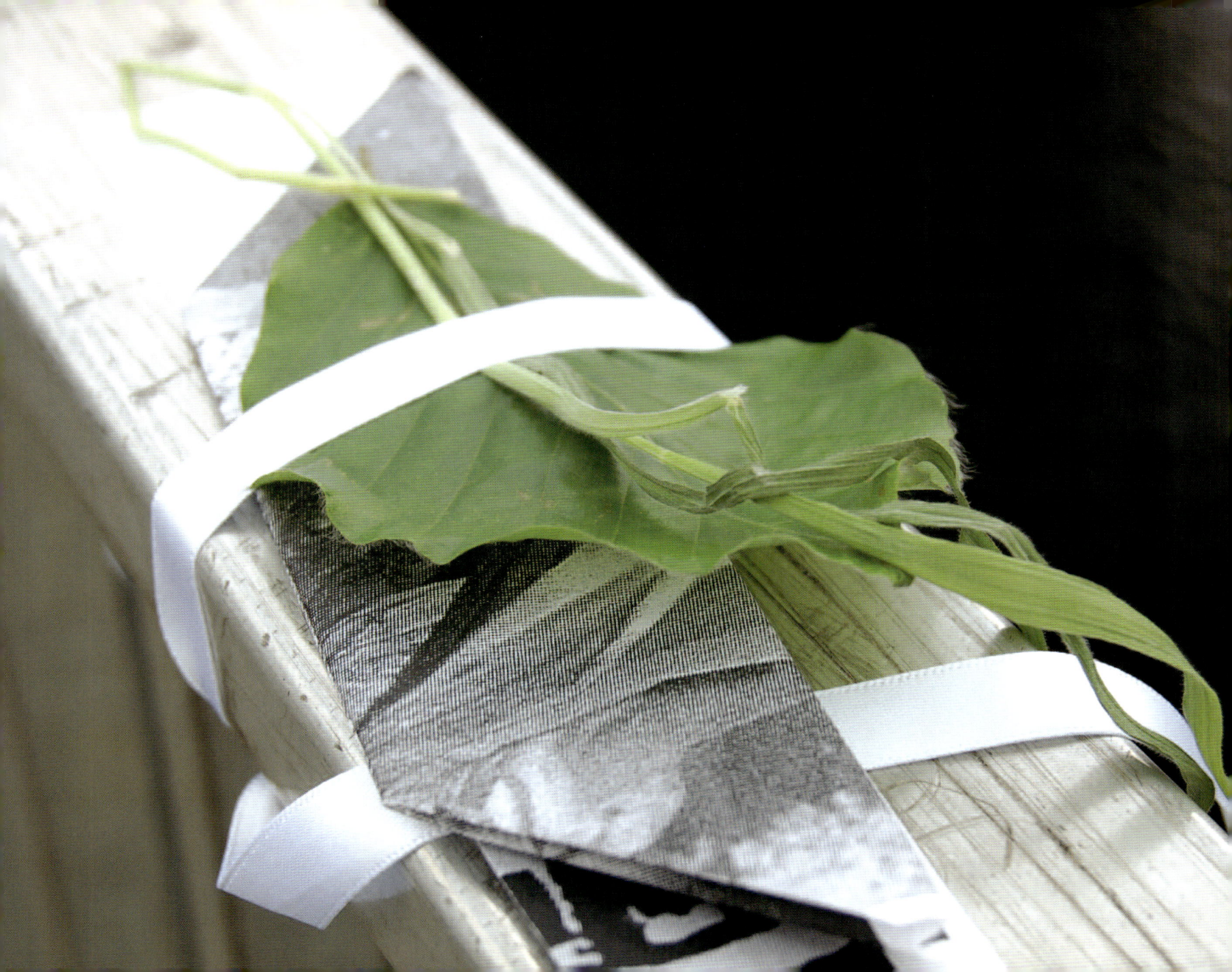

Bobby C. Alexander

Public Art in the Ritual Construction of Human Community

This text has been adapted from the paper presented at the symposium held during *Holy Hiatus*. It includes a dialogue between Alexander and the audience that has been transcribed from an audio recording.

Ritual is a liminal social process, one that temporarily suspends the social conventions, norms and roles guiding participants' everyday social relationships and exchanges, namely their assigned social statuses and social identities that ordinarily distinguish them from one another. What is more, as a form of liminality, ritual invites participants to imagine and create new roles, identities and ways of relating and interacting, in particular ones that are more communitarian. Drawing upon anthropologist Victor Turner's theory of ritual as an agent of human community, this paper illustrates the transformative capacity of theatre performance as a form of ritual liminality by offering as a case study Jerzy Grotowski's Polish Laboratory Theatre. The paper goes on to explore the performance art created for *Holy Hiatus* as ritual liminality and communitas, examining the social context – everyday social-structural roles, identities, and relationships and interchanges – out of which the art performances emerge, the impact of the art on the wider social context – how the performances transform everyday social relationships and interactions, or have the potential to create communitarian exchanges and relations, how the art engages the community – and how it might be considered 'holy'. All are themes on which the symposium focused.

Celf Gyhoeddus yn Adeiladwaith Defodol y Gymuned Ddynol

Addasiad o'r papur a gyflwynwyd yn y symposiwm a gynhaliwyd yn ystod *Holy Hiatus* yw'r testun hwn. Mae'n cynnwys trafodaeth rhwng Alexander a'r gynulleidfa, wedi ei thrawsgrifio o recordiad sain.

Proses gymdeithasol drothwyol yw defod, proses sydd yn atal dros dro gonfensiynau cymdeithasol, arferion, a rolau sydd yn llywio perthnasau a chysylltiadau cymdeithasol cyffredin y sawl sy'n cymryd rhan, sef eu statws a'u hunaniaethau cymdeithasol dynodedig sydd fel arfer yn eu gwahaniaethu oddi wrth ei gilydd. Yn ogystal, oherwydd eu bod yn drothwyol, mae defodau'n gwahodd cyfranogwyr i ddychmygu a chreu rolau a hunaniaethau newydd, a ffyrdd newydd o ymwneud ag eraill, a hynny mewn ffordd fwy cymunedol. Gan dynnu ar ddamcaniaeth yr anthropolegydd Victor Turner o'r ddefod fel asiant y gymuned ddynol, mae'r papur hwn yn dangos grym trawsffurfiol perfformiadau theatrig fel math ar drothwyoledd defodol drwy gynnig astudiaeth achos o Theatr Labordy Jerzy Grotowski o Wlad Pwyl. Yna, bydd y papur yn archwilio'r perfformiadau celfyddydol a grëwyd ar gyfer *Holy Hiatus* o safbwynt trothwyoledd defodol a *communitas*, ac yn archwilio'r cyd-destun cymdeithasol – rolau cymdeithasol-strwythurol arferol, hunaniaethau, a pherthynas ac ymwneud ag eraill – y mae'r perfformiadau celfyddydol yn deillio ohonynt. Edrychir hefyd ar effaith y gwaith celf ar y cyd-destun cymdeithasol ehangach – sut mae'r perfformiadau yn trawsnewid perthnasau a chysylltiadau cymdeithasol arferol, eu gallu i greu perthnasau a chysylltiadau cymunedol, sut mae'r gelfyddyd yn tynnu'r gymuned i mewn – a sut y gellid ei hystyried yn "sanctaidd." Dyma themâu yr oedd y symposiwm yn canolbwyntio arnynt.

I have been asked to talk about ritual as a liminal social event or process, which is to say, one that temporarily suspends the social conventions, norms and roles guiding participants' everyday social exchanges, namely their assigned social statuses and social identities that ordinarily distinguish them from one another, and consequently one that invites them to imagine and create new ones. As a result, ritual allows people to encounter one another in a qualitatively different way from that governed by the routines, regulations and roles that mediate their everyday social interchanges. Ritual allows interchanges that are more direct and spontaneous. Moreover, ritual creates an opportunity for people to experience a more basic form of human community underlying their social-structural ties, which are 'artificial', because these are social constructs.[1] The experience of ritual community has the potential to transform people's everyday social relations, to make them more communitarian, if only temporarily.

I will draw upon British anthropologist Victor Turner's explanation of ritual's transformative capacity to alter existing social structures and social relations, making them more communitarian. I met Turner, and later corresponded with him, while writing my doctoral dissertation devoted to his theory of ritual as an agent of social change. Turner died of a heart attack while I was writing. Richard Schechner introduced me to Turner when Schechner invited him to address his class on 'Performance Theory' in the Tisch School of the Arts at New York University (NYU). Schechner had invited me to audit his course while I was a PhD student of Religious Studies and social-scientific study of religion at Columbia University and also at Union Theological Seminary in New York many years ago.

In addition, I have been asked to comment on ritual and liminal dimensions of the public art created for *Holy Hiatus*. It goes without saying that the art takes on a life of its own and generates manifold possibilities of meaning. Whether intended or not, the art, as human creative action, is a form of liminality; it suspends conventions and rules that define and place boundaries upon the everyday and the ordinary, encouraging creativity, ambiguity and unbounded possibility in reconfiguring the elements of ordinary life and creating new possibilities, and the art invites viewers, or participants, to do the same. Being liminal, the artwork also invites exploration and creation of a form of human community that differs from everyday social relations because communitarian relations are unbounded by social convention and norms, and hence, are spontaneous and direct. All five art performances – by Alastair MacLennan, Maura Hazelden, Simon Whitehead, Anna Lucas and Yvonne Buchheim – have ritual and liminal, particularly communitarian, features, even those that at first appear to be solitary or distant, in the case of the film, which actually involves viewers as participants. All of the art invites individual viewers to participate in the work by imaginatively reconfiguring the everyday, and by literally becoming a part of the artwork, or creating the work. Neither are viewers or members of the audience involved as solitary participants. All of the art invites us to participate in or create the work as members of a kind of community of people participating in or creating the work.

It also goes without saying that the art performances invite awareness of psychological aspects of human identity and human experience broadly conceived that are shared – solitariness and connectedness to others, having a self and being/performing different selves before others, for example – as well as awareness of differences that exist among human beings and across human experiences. Related to these are the philosophical issues about human nature and identity the art also invites us to consider. Moving beyond these issues of human identity and experience, I draw upon sociology, the academic discipline within which I practice, to invite us to explore how the art performances might express and/or address aspects of human social identity and social experience. What elements of social-structural identity and social status might the artworks make us aware of and invite us to consider? What is the wider social and social-structural context of the art? What social realities or social forces frame and inform the art and help to motivate and shape it? How might the art make an impact on its social context or everyday social-structural exchanges? How does the art engage the community? Do its ritual dimensions create opportunities to experience human community in ways not always experienced within the wider social context? Returning to the theme of the art projects and symposium, I also invite us to explore how these experiences might be holy. In the spirit of ritual liminality and of the performative and participatory nature of the art performances, I will ask us as the audience for, or participants in, the work to answer these questions together after we free associate our thoughts and feelings about the work.

Turner's Theory of Ritual as Agent of Social Change

Since time immemorial, human beings have engaged in ritual and in public creative acts as ritual in order to construct community. Participants in ritual and public acts have recognized that both create a variety of forms of community, from proscribed forms that impose social statuses and roles promoting existing social institutions – both those that are beneficent and liberating, such as democratic government, and oppressive, such as totalitarian regimes – to more spontaneous forms, such as rituals of role reversal. At the same time participants have experienced ritual community of a more basic, open, and equalitarian form, one they have carried over into their everyday social interactions to transform existing social institutions, making restrictive and oppressive ones less so and more liberating.

Examples include political protests from Gdansk to Berlin agitating for the end of state communism, and liturgical renewal in the Catholic Church and more recently Catholic 'base communities' in Latin America.

While participants in ritual long ago discovered ritual's capacity to encourage such social transformations, scholars have analysed ritual's capacity only more recently. Turner, whose work took him from ritual in African lineage societies to contemporary experimental theatre, is generally recognized as the first to articulate a theory of ritual's ability to transform along communitarian lines existing social structures, and the social relationships and interchanges they regulate or inform. Turner argued that ritual's capacity to transform society is innate; it lies in ritual's nature as a liminal process and in the communitarian exchanges it fosters.

Turner built upon the observations of the Belgian ethnologist Arnold Van Gennep, who had observed that rites of passage are a transitional process moving participants from a former social status, social identity and social role to a new one.[2] Van Gennep noted that in order to assign the new status, identity and role of adult to those adolescents undergoing puberty in traditional societies, ritual first separates initiates from the former status, identity and roles they held as children. This renders initiates' social placement, identity and role ambiguous as they undergo a transition to the status of adult and the new identity and roles assigned them once they are reincorporated into society, now as adults, at the conclusion of ritual initiation. Van Gennep applied the Latin term *limen*, which translates as 'threshold', to the transition stage in rites of passage in order to characterize the relationship between initiates and their elders, as well as that among themselves, as liminal, which is to say, social-structurally ambiguous and hence full of possibility regarding social status and identity.

Turner further developed Van Gennep's observations by noting that ambiguity of ritual participants' social status and identity can encourage the creation of new ones, including those that are unexpected and not entirely within the control of elders or authorities in charge of ritual. Ritual places participants in a state of 'suspended animation' or 'a kind of [social-structural] limbo'; they are 'betwixt and between' social statuses and identities.[3] Free of their social obligation to conform their social interactions to the expectations and obligations of their 'quotidian' roles and identities, participants are able to rearrange elements of their social statuses and identities, and to imagine and create new ones. In Turner's view, ritual liminality is 'subjunctive'; it allows consideration of the question, 'What if?'

Furthermore, Turner noted that the interchanges between participants who are momentarily freed of their ordinary social statuses and identities are qualitatively different from their daily exchanges. Participants' encounters with one another in ritual liminality are not mediated by the social statuses and roles that ordinarily apply, because these have been temporarily 'suspended' by ritual liminality. As a result, they are free to experience one another more directly and spontaneously, and as equals. Their encounters have the quality of 'I–Thou' relationships.[4] Their social bonds are not the result of socially proscribed behaviours and social routines. Rather, ritual 'grounds' the bond among participants in their experience of community with one another. In order to distinguish the different quality of ritual community from that created by everyday social structure, Turner referred to the former as 'communitas'.

In Turner's view, ritual's liminal nature – ritual suspends social structure as it makes a transition – and its innate capacity to create communitas – as a result, participants are free to be direct and spontaneous with one another – make it essentially 'anti-structure'. Together, ritual liminality and ritual communitas constitute 'ritual anti-structure'. As anti-structure, ritual is 'subversive' of social structure. Turner understood ritual to emerge in response to the lack of communitarian experiences or diminishment of them within existing social structures. The latter leave no or little room for spontaneous and direct social exchanges as they regulate social interactions in the promotion of routine, scripted exchanges, and through these, maintain the social-structural status quo. Turner argued that human beings have an equal need for structure in their social relations and for freedom from structure experienced as communitarian relations. As equal human social needs, albeit with different social purposes, social structure and communitas exist in 'dialectical relation' to one another.

From Turner's point of view, the ideal purpose of ritual is to 'infuse' everyday social structure with communitarian purpose, 'to place social structure in the service of human community'. Turner's main contribution is his observation that the experience of ritual community alters the quality of participants' daily social interchanges even after ritual has assigned new statuses and roles and reincorporated them in the social structure in place, making their daily exchanges, along with the existing social structure, more communitarian, or having the potential to do so. Turner offered the example of ritual role reversal: even in the moment the chief of the African lineage society is being crowned, having been ritually humbled or temporarily given the low status of a village commoner before being exalted, he is reminded that his office exists to serve the people and the common good.

Turner argued that, given ritual's liminal nature and its inherent capacity to create communitas, it has 'ontological status'. That is to say, ritual does not merely reflect or express social structure; ritual liminality and communitas are 'generative' of new social structures, ones that are more communitarian, if fleetingly. Ritual liminality generates new ideas, symbols, images, social-structural arrangements and identities; ritual communitas generates the experience of human community and more communitarian social structures. Ritual's generative status is evident in its transformation of existing social structures.

Turner took a radical view of ritual as social transformation, arguing that all forms of ritual have the potential to undermine existing social structure, given ritual's liminal, or anti-structural, nature and the anti-structural essence of ritual communitas. These include rituals that are tightly controlled by power structures that utilise ritual in order to maintain or conserve the social-structural status quo by reinforcing or imposing existing social statuses, roles and identities. When rituals maintain the status quo, their anti-structural features have been 'corralled' by power structures and the experience of communitas has been narrowly 'circumscribed'.

Thus, Turner turned our usual way of thinking about ritual on its head. Ahead of Turner, the prevailing view of ritual, held by Bronislaw Malinowski and A.R. Radcliffe-Brown, among other structural-functionalist anthropologists, understood ritual's fundamental role to be that of maintaining the social-structural status quo. While Turner believed the structural-functional theory of ritual has some validity, he pointed out its limitations. These begin with the inability of the theory to account for the social changes encouraged by rituals, and to take into account ritual's potential to transform existing social structures along communitarian lines.

As an aside, I note that Catherine Bell, a student of ritual within religious studies, has argued that ritual has no fundamental or essential purpose, and that it is put to various and conflicting purposes in any given time, place, or in any given circumstances in order to accomplish specific and changing goals and aims.[5] Her view reminds us of the contemporary postmodern discussion of and debate about human 'nature', human universals or givens, shared human meanings; indeed, whether or not meaning is possible.

Turner constructed his theory of ritual based on his ethnographic observations of traditional ritual within African lineage societies before applying them to traditional forms of ritual elsewhere – for example, pilgrimage in Mexico and other places – as well as to contemporary ritual theatre and performance. Turner's theory helps to illumine a variety of forms of performative art and theatre, on which he commented extensively late in his career. He appreciated the ritual dimensions of contemporary theatre and performance for their serious, although playful, or liminal, role in reconsidering human social-structural identity, critiquing social institutions and society, and creating human community.[6] Turner coined the term 'liminoid' in order to distinguish expressions of ritual liminality in Western society, such as theatre, from ritual in 'tribal' societies, which, he noted, are essentially conservative, and in order to call attention to the pronounced individualism and voluntary basis of Western society and theatre. The later qualities distinguish the audience from playwright and actors; audience members make their own judgements about the performance and the ideological views represented. 'Liminoid' further distinguishes Western theatre as critical of the existing social order; Turner considered the basic purpose of tribal ritual to be to advance the purposes of everyday social structure, which is to organize society to meet its material needs.

Curiously, Turner did not specifically address sacred or holy dimensions of liminality and communitas, or those of contemporary theatre and performance, or of theatre in general. (We will return to the concept of the holy.) The roots of theatre in religious or sacred ritual are well known; such ritual is said to redress conflict within a divine, cosmic or ultimate context by acting out the conflict and, in the process, resolving or transforming it.[7] Turner understood the roots of theatre to lie more particularly in 'the social drama', or 'social process', which by nature is conflictual, since social structure creates social division and inequality, and since it exists in tension with an equal need for community.[8] Specifically, theatre arose as a redressive ritual performance that enacts the social conflict underlying the social drama and resolves it by transforming the existing social structure, making it more communitarian. Given ritual and theatre's redressive role within the social drama, these forms of liminality or 'human play' are serious.[9]

Turner appreciated the sacred dimension of his subject matter – African, Mexican or other traditional religious rituals – the object of which is the divine, cosmic or ultimate reality. Turner might accept the term 'holy' to characterise the liminal features of contemporary performative art, given the fact that, in response to an attempt by students at New York University to recreate tribal ritual that Turner had observed in Africa, he described 'living ritual' as having something 'numinous', and even 'dangerous', 'in the atmosphere'.[10]

Grotowski's Polish Laboratory Theatre

An avowed anti-Marxist and nominal Anglican, Turner was critical of perhaps the best-known example of secular contemporary theatre – Jerzy Grotowski's Polish Laboratory Theatre. Grotowski is credited with extending the attempts of theatre directors earlier in the twentieth century to involve the audience in novel ways in theatre performance. For his innovations, he was lauded by the Polish Communist Party. Turner viewed Grotowski's theatrical experiments, such as *Night Vigil*, as the imposition of a rigid, quasi-

dogmatic ideology manifest in a narrow communalism of the cognoscenti, as opposed to open communitas. We could apply Turner's concept of 'normative communitas' to his view of Grotowski's theatre. Turner proposed that communitas cannot be identified with any specific social structure, nor any specific form or instance of human community, since it is by nature anti-structure. Furthermore, as a liminal phenomenon, communitas is unpredictable and cannot be controlled. Attempts to promote a specific form or instance of community, one that is identified with a particular social structure, as normative for other people and

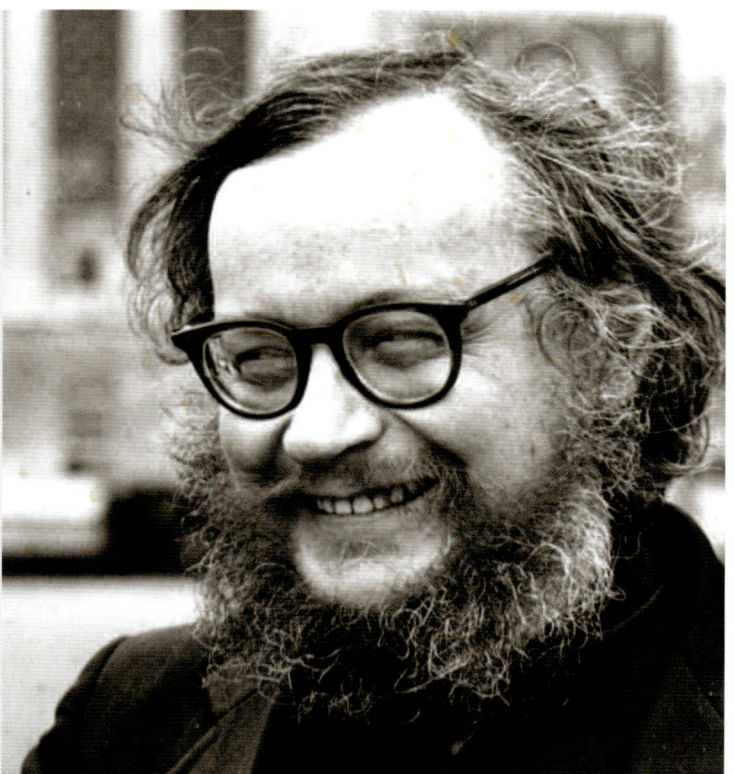

occasions are merely narrow or limited expressions of communitas.

Grotowski's ideal for his theatrical experiments was that they give birth to a new social order that would replace conventional Western society and its routine and mechanical social exchanges. Grotowski articulated his ideal for his experiments as social reform in numerous lectures – several of which I attended in New York – videos, and publications.[11] The experiments, like the one in which I participated, described below, generate communitarian exchanges that are not necessarily channelled into a social programme to reform society, but create more immediate and momentary experiences of communitas. I participated in experimental workshops with members of Grotowki's theatre company held at NYU and in New York's SoHo art district. These were unscripted, open-ended exchanges between participants who voluntarily engaged one another. The workshops were devoid of overt ideology. Clearly the workshops fit within Grotowski's larger ideological framework; nevertheless, they were liminal throughout, resisting ideology and a programme of specific social reform.

The week-long workshop in SoHo in which I participated included around ten participants who were led by two members of the Polish Laboratory Theatre, one of them Jacek Zymslowski. Among the participants were NYU graduate students in the arts and actors and a dancer associated with small performance companies in New York. Each workshop, held on a separate day, lasted around four or five hours. We were instructed ahead of our arrival to wear loose-fitting clothing. During the initial session, the members of Grotowksi's company taught us a series of five or six martial arts and yoga-like movements. These were designed to quiet the mind and put us in touch with our bodies, particularly with parts of our bodies people do not ordinarily use to express themselves and communicate with others, including our backs, buttocks, chests and abdomens. All of the work undertaken as an individual, a member of a pair, and of a group was performed in silence. The workshop leaders had instructed the group to perform in silence in order to break through the limitations of speech and encourage using the body to communicate with others in the group.

After performing the movement exercises as a group, participants repeated them on their own, using them as a kind of runway to be more experimental and creative in expressing themselves and communicating with their bodies. At the point when each participant felt free from social conventions and inhibitions, she or he moved about freely. Participants explored their bodies, expressed themselves through their bodies in new ways and used their bodies in unexpected ways to connect to and communicate with other participants. Participants worked alone, with another participant or a workshop leader and in groups. During the initial training session, the workshop leaders commented on how well participants had or had not broken free of social convention and body habits in expressing themselves and communicating with one another.

Working as a group over the week, opening up to one another and making intimate physical contact created a strong bond among members of the group. At the same time that participants experienced community among themselves, they commented that they experienced people outside of the workshop, including strangers, in a different way. Leaving the workshops and re-entering the everyday social world of New York, I looked at people on the sidewalks and subways differently; I looked at them as fellow human beings with whom I might experience a bond in a ritual or liminal event, if only momentarily, if the right opportunity arose.

Grotowski's experiments in which there was no separate

audience – everyone participated – were distinct from the earlier conventional plays with scripts and an audience. Although I never witnessed any of Grotowski's more conventional plays, such as *The Constant Prince*, I have read about them and seen photos and videos, most recently those in the exhibit *A Theater without Theater*, on the theatre of revolt against theatre convention held at Barcelona's Museum of Contemporary Art in summer 2007. I can well imagine that members of the audience also experienced or approximated the experience of liminality and communitas encouraged by actors who were in a state of 'flow', to borrow Turner's description of the contemporary theatre actor who transcends both training and spontaneity.[12] By report, Ryzsard Cieslak, a member of Grotowski's company who played *The Constant Prince*, appeared to be in such a state. 'Flow' is close to Antonin Artaud's ideal of the actor 'signaling [to the audience] through the flames', his metaphor for making the transcendent – the world of ideas and imagination that have the potential to transform reality – real within the theatre, and, through it, real within ordinary life.[13] Experiences of actors and audiences transcending ordinary consciousness and identities in a heightened awareness that humans are bound together in the common experience of tension between manifold limitations and unbounded possibility have led many observers of contemporary theater to characterize it as 'holy theatre'.[14]

This leads us to the theme of our symposium – *Holy Hiatus* – and to the public art created in association with it. Given his interest in the ritual dimensions of theatre and performance art in his own British and other Western cultures, Turner would have appreciated the ritual, liminal and communitarian dimensions of the art performances, especially their capacity to generate new experiences in which everyday social life and social exchanges are transformed as we are invited to reinvision them, and to create experiences of

human community. Turner's observation that the playfulness of performance in contemporary Western society has a serious role in the social drama of everyday life reminds us of the potential of the art performances to transform everyday social exchanges.

Ritual Experiment/Ritual of Greeting
Now I would like us to experiment together, to create our own ritual allowing us to participate in the artworks in a different way and on a different level. No one should feel pressured to participate. You are free to remain seated and silent. We'll begin with a ritual of greeting.[15] You are free to greet one another however you wish. I'll begin. I'm a Texan, and in Texas we greet people like this. *(Alexander walks a short distance to a woman he does not know who is seated on the front row. He bends over her, stretches out both of his arms, and places his arms and hands behind her back in an embrace while he places his right cheek against her left one. She accepts his hug. Members of the audience laugh. Many in the audience get up from their seats and greet one another in a variety of ways. Laughter and animated conversation continue. Professor Iain Biggs playfully says to Alexander, 'Now that you've let the genie out of the bottle, how will you get it back in?' Alexander has already informed the audience that they will be asked to share their responses to the art.)*

Holy Hiatus Artists
The public artworks created by Alastair MacLennan, Maura Hazelden, Simon Whitehead, Anna Lucas and Yvonne Buchheim create in us a heightened awareness of aspects of humanity that are shared and of human experiences that are common to all of us. What is more, they create experiences of human community with other participants, who include passers-by, who may not be aware

that they are participating in and helping to create the performances. This heightened awareness and experience have the quality of the holy, a subject to which we will return. The art performances invite us to interact with other participants, including passers-by, and with people on film in ways that are outside social convention and routine, to be more direct and spontaneous, and to experience community with them, even after returning to the everyday world, if only momentarily.

Ruth Jones has asked us collectively to consider how arts practitioners can engage communities through ritual, and how liminal identities might be explored through public art that engages ritual, among other questions. I'd like us to return to her question about engaging communities after starting with the sociological ones I raised earlier. First I'd like us to free associate images, thoughts, and feelings in a word or a few words for any one or all of the performances we experienced in order to allow our images, thoughts and feelings to guide us as we answer.

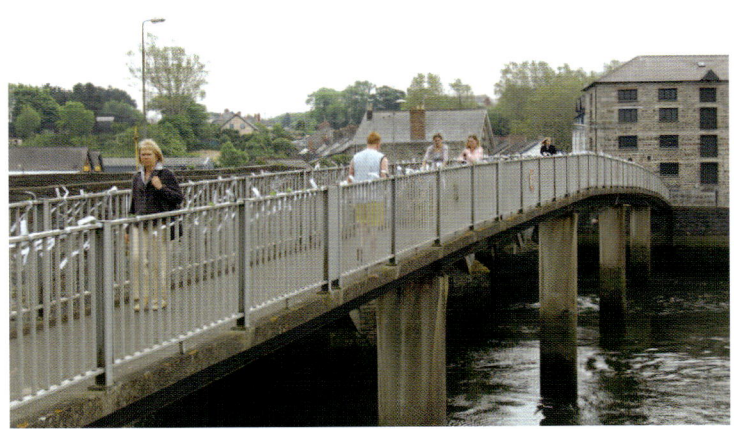

Alexander begins:
Evocative
A mother rocks her child on her hip as swimmers swim and singers sing.

Audience members respond:
Is that man on the bridge official?
Fluid
Watching from inside a bubble
What a wonderful sound!
Endurance
Celebratory
Curiosity
Usual and unusual
Emotion
Exhaustion (says Alexander)
Vulnerability and embarrassment
Exhilaration – new energy (Alexander)
Out of the ordinary
For a spilt second I didn't know whether the swimmers were dead or alive.

Alexander: *Now I'd like us to return to my sociological questions. What aspects of social-structural identity do these artworks, their practitioners and participants express and/or address beyond philosophical and psychological issues of human identity? By social-structural identity sociology means, for example, social status, class, ethnicity, dominant group, subordinate group, insider, outsider, deviant, age group, biological sex, gender and other identities society assigns us and we voluntarily adopt.*

Audience Member 1: *I was thinking about the bridge with the ribbons… how it was usual in that it could be a Fair day or something special happening, he was all dressed in black so he kind of looked like he might be official… but he looked quite strange, his clothes weren't quite official, maybe from a different era, there was grass as well as ribbons, that was a bit unusual, so it had usual and unusual aspects about it, so it was normal in that you could still walk across the bridge, but this man was decorating it in an unusual way, so you knew it, and you didn't know it, and you weren't sure what you were part of.*

Alexander: *So some ambiguity of social identity? Of social status or social placement?*

Audience Member 2: *I think someone responded to your earlier request that it was out of the ordinary – we seek that out of the ordinary, while we wish also to have a security or foundation of the ordinary. So ritual in itself allows us to sustain the ordinary, but also to seek and recognize something which is out of the ordinary.*

Audience Member 3: *… and to feel safe, like it isn't too intrusive or frightening – the ribbons on the bridge, it's not too threatening.*

Audience Member 1: *Something about needing an open space, like Maura and Lou's piece. That was also usual as well in some ways, it was almost like church, it was very still, you had physical shifts in the feelings about the space that they created, but because it wasn't like something you knew, it was a bit different, yes, it was being in that open space of a bit different. So it's a bit edgy.*

Alexander: *People are both recognizable, as they are using our societal filter to assume their identities and roles, and yet, and you*

put this in an eloquent way, there's something unfamiliar about them and something unfamiliar about myself as I catch myself in this act of reflexivity – being myself and not myself at the same time.*

Alexander: *Do the ritual dimensions of the artwork create opportunities to experience human community in ways not always experienced within the wider social context?*

Audience Member 4: *I haven't seen most of the works actually, but I would ask the question, do you have to be familiar with an art language to engage with some of these things? We are people who have that language, what about people who are just walking about in the town or haven't got that language, how do they see it?*

Ruth Jones: *I'm not sure that a lot of people read it as art, who didn't know about the project, who just happened to see it, that's the impression that I've got from overhearing what other people have said, that they didn't necessarily interpret it as art, and the artists didn't necessarily present it in that way either.*

Audience Member 4: *So what did they think they were doing? Did they just think they were weird!?*

Jones: *I think there was a lot of curiosity, why are they doing this? I think people were looking for an explanation, but they didn't necessarily go to art for it.*

Audience Member 5: *My only experience of this stuff was a brief observation yesterday as I drove over the road bridge, while the ribbons were being tied onto the footbridge and there was a family walking across the bridge, and there was just that sense of things going on around them that were slightly beyond their comprehension, part of that stuff that happens anyway, the environment's being changed all the time, I don't have anything to do with it – or do I? I'll pretend not to notice…*

Alexander: *It appears that there were quite a few takers as I moved from performance to performance, people who stood on the edge and others who walked right on through it.*

Audience Member 6: *I've seen a few people looking but pretending that they're not looking.*

Alexander: *Some more sociological questions: What is the wider social context of the art? What social realities or social forces frame the art and help to motivate it and even shape it? Sociology says that we don't escape social institutions. We're socialized. The primary agents of this are our family, religion and so forth.*

Iain Biggs: *In relation to some of the other questions you've asked, one of the things that it might do is ask whether our sense of community is limited to the human.*

Alexander: *Yes, I'm glad you mentioned that point, many of the works include human and animal interaction plus engagement with being on a living organism.*

Audience Member 7: *I'm not sure which question I'm responding to but I was interested in the same theme and I was struck by Anna Lucas's work, and it reflected a vital part of this community with the video of the farming, and the young person with the sheep, and it was very very strong, and very much about the inner life, this is what this*

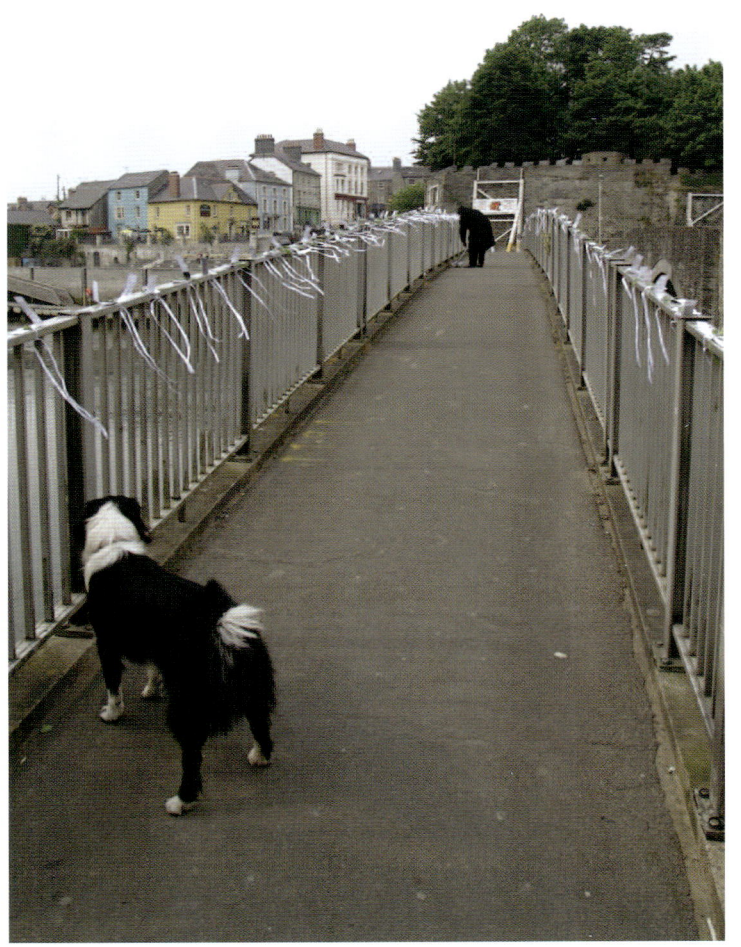

community was. And there's a lot of us who have moved here, and that has changed that community, but it's a farming community really.

Alexander (talking to Anna Lucas): *You've pointed out elsewhere that humans have domesticated animals. [The young boy] is both socialised as farmer, in a tradition that is passed on of domesticating animals. At the same time, I was impressed that there was almost a respectful recognition of the otherness of the animal kingdom, which perhaps in some ways is disruptive of a relationship of domestication.*

Biggs: *There are interesting arguments to suggest that actually animals have domesticated us, and certainly my cat would agree!*

Alexander (Nodding his head in order to say 'Yes'): *This is a lot of fun isn't it?! It's been a long time since I have lived and worked among artists, so this is a great pleasure. In the interest of time, we'll move on. How might the art make an impact on its social context or impact everyday social exchanges? (Addressing an audience member) You said some people didn't know what to make of the art, that they participate sometimes unwillingly.*

Audience Member 8: *That in itself is a point of discussion, people have been involved in it and they don't know what they've been involved in, and then the next day in the shops they say 'what was going on?' That in itself will make people talk to each other, who maybe wouldn't talk to each other otherwise.*

Jones: *I think it raised questions about behaviour, and what kind of behaviour is acceptable in social or public situations. I think somebody made a comment that the work was relatively safe, so it allowed for this kind of flexibility of what social behaviour is OK,*

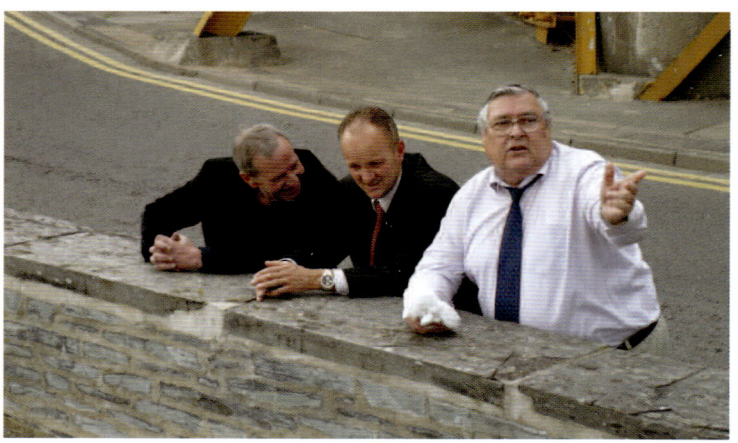

without people feeling that they have to retreat into a much safer set of ideas about identity, perhaps.

Maura Hazelden: *On a very personal level from my own performance, it has expanded the communication I have with several people who I go to a meditation group with who came to the performance. They somehow understood something more about me, it just has broadened our communication.*

Audience Member 7: *That was the point I wanted to make about Anna Lucas's work, it was communication with that part of this community, suddenly they have become part of the art world.*

Yvonne Buchheim: *I would probably say a similar thing from having been in the swimming pool for a few days. When I approached people first it was always like a running joke of the art, like what do you want? Or what are you doing here? We have nothing to do with it, in a way, and then through the days of being there things have changed, attitudes have changed, suddenly sparks of interest have occurred.*

Audience Member 9: *Can I just ask a question? Why are we talking about art as if it's separate from life? As if it's something other that we do? What was interesting about Alastair's work was that it was perceived as work. There was a bunch of older guys talking about it as if it was work, not as art. So it's interesting why we always separate art from life.*

Alexander: *By social convention. I refer to some theoreticians including those who are art practitioners who speak about when art is life. Turner has a wonderful flow chart between social drama and performative theatre – a figure eight turned on its side with arrows flowing from the one half to the other, so that the two are not ever separate.*[16] *Moving on in the interest of time: How are these experiences holy? I realise that I didn't offer a generalised definition of 'holy'. My one mention of it was specific to comments on experimental theatre in the 60s and 70s.*

Audience Member 10: *They're mediated by priests.*

Alexander: *Are they? Is art making a special work? Can we all make art?*

Biggs: *All forms of work are special to the people who carry them out and in that sense of specialness is something that in a very open sense could be referred to as a heightening of attention,* (addressing Alexander) *you used the word 'numinous', maybe that corresponds to this?*

Hazelden: *Not all things holy are mediated by anyone.*

Audience Member 11: *Is it something about the intensity, the intensity of the focus that makes it have something holy about it?*

Audience Member 12: *Of course it's about semantics as well because if you use the word 'holy' in contemporary society, traditionally the word 'holy' was allied to religion, and organised religions accompanying the state, and if we live in a country whereby the official religion of the country diminished so much, especially over the last fifty years, so people are looking for other forms of spiritual development or spiritual questioning. So if we're living in that society today, then the word 'holy' might be looking at something which is outside of the church, or outside of religion, which might offer some kind of solution to a spiritual problem.*

Audience Member 2: *Or even outside of the ordinary, that seems to be crucial and a fulcrum of what we're talking about – there is the ordinary that we all perceive, and there are certain things which differ – lift us above the ordinary, or out of the ordinary.*

Audience Member 13: *What if everything is holy?*

Hazelden: *It's the act of perception that changes it.*

Simon Whitehead: *Is it that holy also has holes in it?* (The audience is caught up in spontaneous laughter.)

Audience Member 12: *It used to be very clear-cut, when you went into a cathedral you were in a sacred space, and when you went outside you were in profane space, and of course it's become a lot more malleable now.*

Audience Member 14: *The whole of culture is a ritual sphere, the entirety of civilisation is a ritual sphere. Holiness takes its meaning from the idea of utility and there's nothing less utilitarian than culture and civilisation and the primary evidence for this is its huge and voracious destructive impact, in which we participate.*

Audience Member 15: *I would say that we use our thoughts and our minds to stretch to what is beyond it, and we're fragmenting it by doing that, you're fragmented into artist, my work, the public. If you're talking about liminality, true liminality it's beyond all that, and sometimes we connect to it through various ways, we're just justifying the act after it's happened, we're gilding the lily.*

Audience Member 16: *The word 'holy' also suggests the referential, as well.*

Audience Member 17: *Something has occurred to me about Cardigan, we have a thing called Barley Saturday where the horses run up and down the street, this is something which is involving the whole community, it's an incredibly emotional event, everybody's there and sometimes I wonder if they realize that its roots are in worshipping Epona, the goddess, for which this particular celebration day probably started. Some things start as a holy thing and then turn into a ritual of repetition, but there's still something there in Barley Saturday that's almost tangible, and it's not just the testosterone of stallions!*

Audience Member 18: *But it's actually getting less and less, over ten years…*

Audience Member 19: *Not at all!*

Audience Member 18: *The intensity has got less and less. At one time it was just stallions tearing up and down the street, now you've got tractors, old cars, the parade is over within ten minutes, and that's what's changed is that intensity of dealing with animals. In film you're looking at an observation of someone else's perception, you're not looking at the real thing. A lot of the talk in here is dealing on the periphery, but we're not in liminality in any sense.*

Audience Member 12: *The intensity of liminal space is dependent on its separation and its being boundaried.*

Alexander: *This is marvellous. Let me move us on!*

How are these experiences holy? None of us has yet fully defined the term, although we have suggested they have the quality of being numinous. Perhaps the best-known study of the 'holy' is Rudolf Otto's *The Idea of the Holy*.[17] I first read this classic work as a graduate student in Religious Studies. A German theologian, who studied the history and phenomenology of religion in comparative context, Otto was interested in the relationship between rational and non-rational aspects of religion, especially those involving religious experience. He was particularly interested in feelings associated with religious experience, which he characterized as a mixture of fear and attraction before the '*mysterium tremendum et fascinans*', the object of such an experience, the mystery before which one is both fearful and drawn in. Otto coined the term *numinous* to refer to meaning that is unique to religious experience, transcends the rational and ethical dimensions of religious experience, and is only experienced existentially. He described the latter as having the feeling of being a creature ('creature feeling') in the presence of a power that is 'wholly other'. In his view, the *mysterium* cannot be approached by way of logic; it can only be approached by way of symbols. Otto's critics charged that the essence of religion and the holy elude attempts to study them phenomenologically.

Otto's definition of the holy is rooted in those provided by the world's religions, which foster experiences of a spiritual reality standing apart from or outside the material world. Religions also seek to understand this reality philosophically as well as engage it aesthetically and ritually. Such a traditionally religious definition of the holy excludes atheist and agnostic artists, including Grotowski and others in experimental theatre. They define the holy in non-religious or non-traditional terms, as an experience of the imagination and ideas as a transcendent reality, along the lines pursued by Artaud. He observed that the transcendent dimension of imagination is not simply that it lies outside ordinary human consciousness: transcendence also lies in the capacity to transform the everyday world. Regardless of claims by world religions that a reality independent of human beings and their imagination in fact exists, both 'sacred' and 'secular' definitions of the holy agree that the holy has a life of its own and, in this, the capacity to operate upon and transform the everyday world.

What does this have to do with performance art, and the art performed ahead of today's symposium? We have seen that performance art has the capacity as ritual to create liminal and communitarian relations, or human community, and to bend these back upon everyday social structure in ways that transform it, if briefly. The 'happenings', 'sit-ins', 'agit-prop', or theatrical political protests, and other ritual performances of the 1960s and 1970s, and the liminal and communitarian relations they engendered transformed ways in which people interacted and related to one another on an individual basis and on a larger social scale. These performances also helped give birth to and became central parts of social protest movements against the Vietnam War, against discrimination inflicted upon blacks, women and other social minorities, against police force used on gays and against their legal discrimination, against traditional marriage and conventional sexual relations, and against other social conventions and institutions supporting the social-structural status quo and traditional society. These and other protest movements promoting more just, egalitarian and communitarian human relations helped to transform society in concrete and long-lasting ways as society, influenced by such social movements, encoded such relations in legislation, laws, court decisions and other legal codes and mandates. We have noted that liminality and communitas give human community a life of its own, which we experience as a force or power, not entirely within our control, transforming our everyday, routine social relations. If we accept as holy the experience of liminality and communitas in acts of artistic creativity as a powerful presence or force beyond our complete control reshaping or having the potential to reshape the everyday world, then performance art plays a significant role in creating experiences of the holy in contemporary, secularised society by creating such transformative liminal and communitarian experiences.

Simon Whitehead

Drift

A series of dance excursions through Cardigan town in collaboration with dancers Kate Willis and Andrea Buckley, photographer Ben Stammers and poet Zoë Skoulding

Wednesday 21st – Friday 23rd May 2008

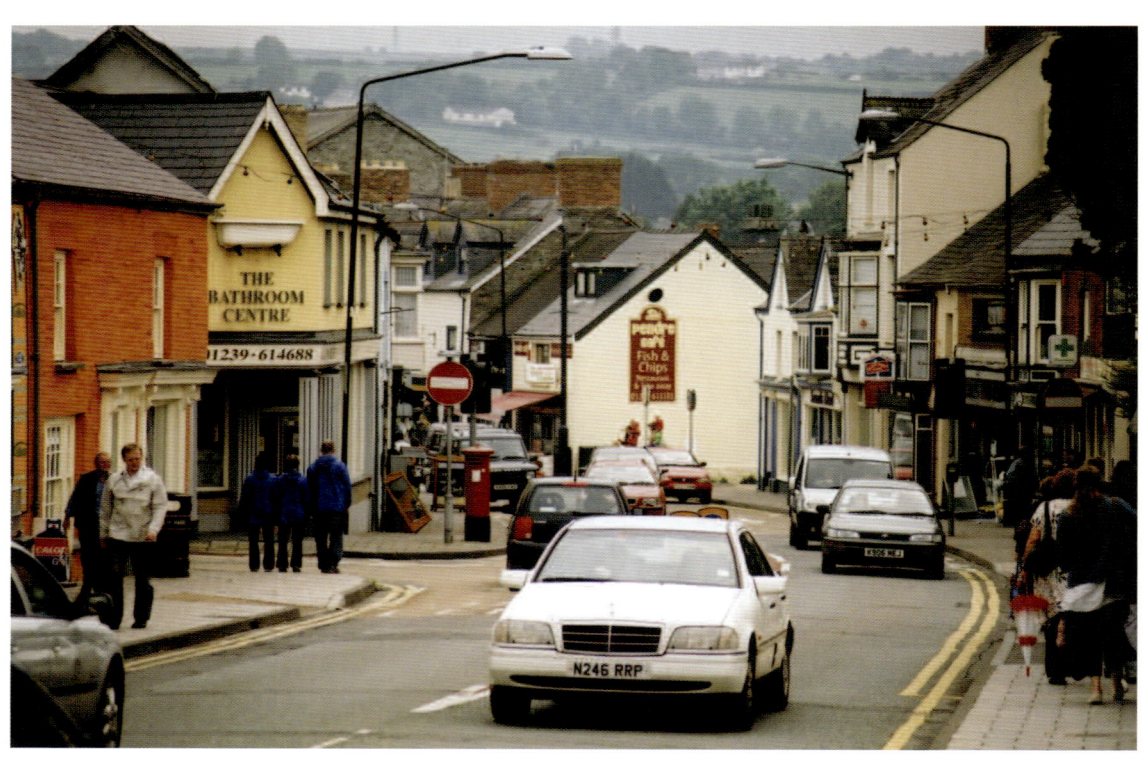

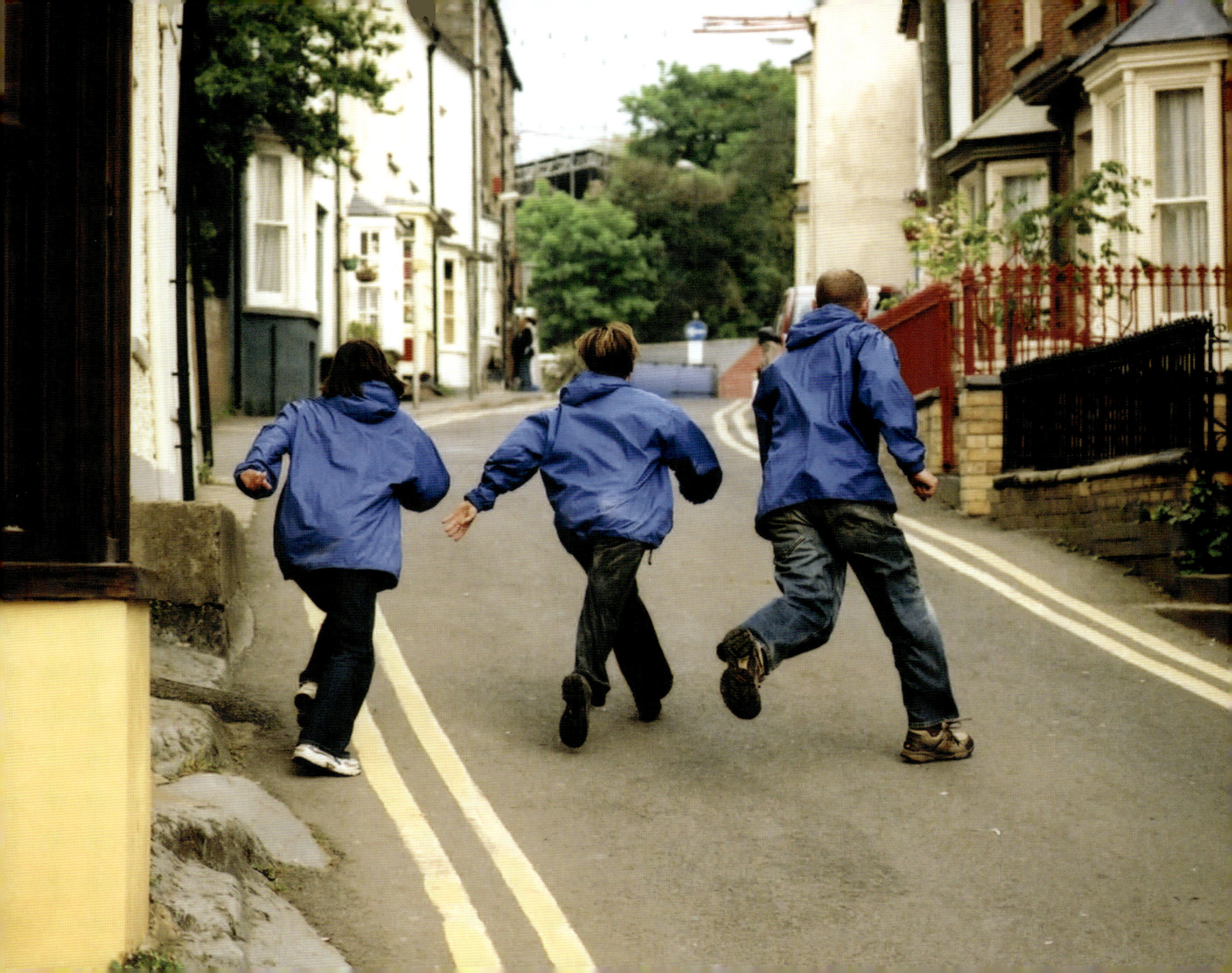

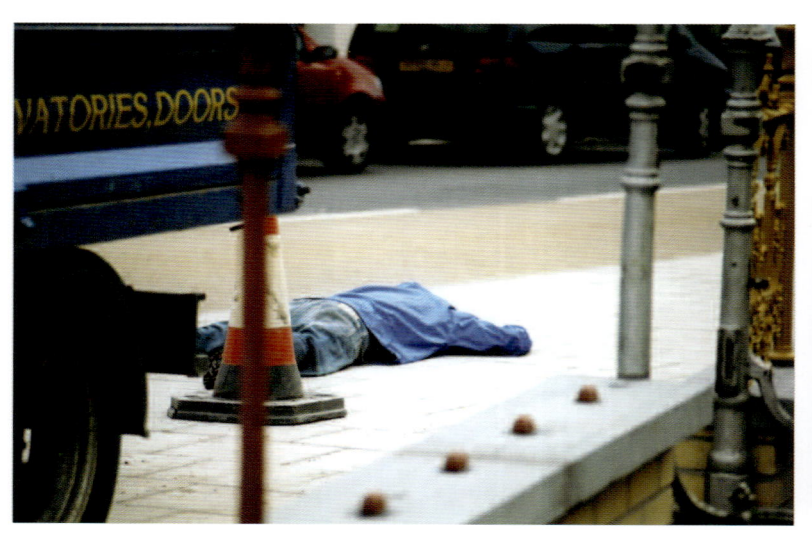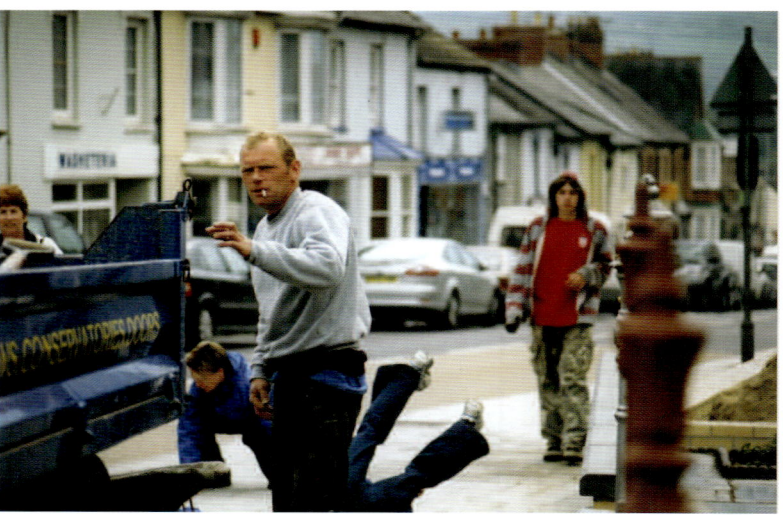

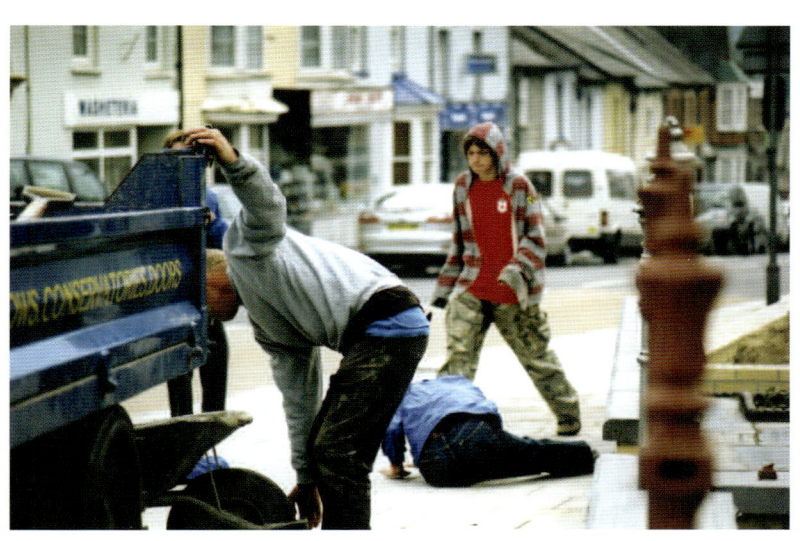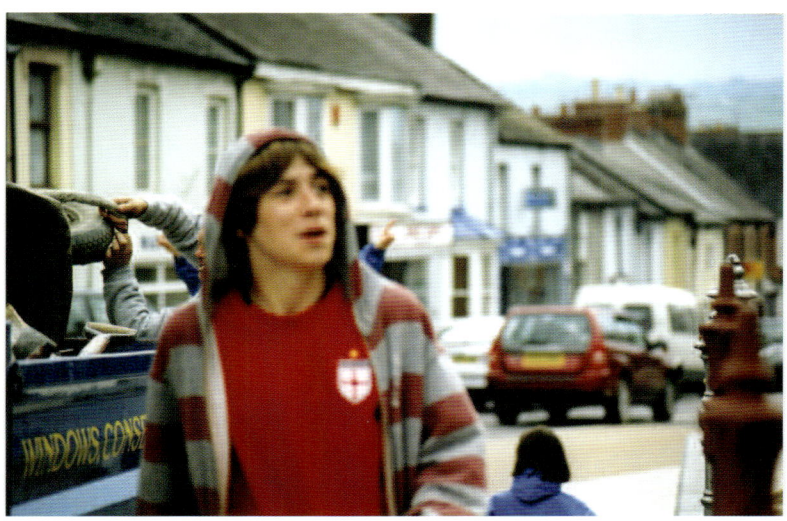

1

A blue figure stands on the bridge wall; a blue figure crouches; a blue figure drips to the ground. Three questions that nobody is answering: no one's even looking. Here in this town. Here on this page, the one through which your eyes swim left, right and down in their pools of salt water.

2

Blue shoots out of the corner of one eye: she spins; the road unravels round her in circles of air and eyes. I can't tell you the shape of this town, only the shape of bodies swivelling round railings, the shape of pebbledash under their fingertips.

3

And where's the blood and guts? Well, here is blood, then: a throb in the soles, heartbeats in footsteps against the pull of work and shopping. A tide of bodies full of blood that shocks with sameness. Here are guts doing what guts do, roads digesting traffic.

4

Oh yes, we're all at work on the same day with its invisible edges of sleep. We are walking to work, or walking is the work of hammering ourselves into the town that wasn't here before, or not the same. Words press over and over into the pages spreading like tarmac.

5

Nowhere's quiet. It's someone's funeral today, one face in everybody's hands, the same words. Their black ties stripe the street; they compose their steps in shades of public grief, torn faces last. When the body's gone the town folds into a handkerchief.

6

They were here a minute ago, she was turning against the shop window rolling its glass around herself. She was caught in the railings, her hood over one eye. She was searching the ground, plucking at asphalt for something she'd lost.

7

He lies down, plays dead or drunk, wrapped in the pavement. Laughter finds its edges and trickles into silence. Infinite cities collide in the stones. The builders lay slabs to hold history down, cementing sediments. One page piles up on another, unreadable.

8

In flesh and blood, language runs along the contours of the street. Have you paid and displayed? Prohibited scaffold, prohibited skip. This is a designated public place. Half-price. Yellow lines swivel under tyres and the page turns back on itself.

9

What is permitted and what is forgotten? What is invited and what is forgiven? And by whom? We write journeys in the streets, fold them up and keep them in pockets. We forget permission. We journey through pockets in the folded streets.

10

On each corner the town he knows turns over in the creases of its map. Birds say the air they own; I ask directions in another language. I am watching and watched as wings touch crumpled buildings. Movements converge in a single lens, shrink to dots and flick upside-down.

11

A monument in limbs and blue nylon becomes flesh against stone. A memory of statues burns outlines in the air. From sentence to sentience. Warped song from speakers in transit. Tidal bodies pent up in electricity: a static charge bursts into movement.

12

The storm weighs on our limbs. Your sinking head. Heat staggers backwards in standstill stop start. Heartbeats overhead in breaking cloud. We run back from the river and the rain runs down our backs in streams where the words break over and over.

Zoë Skoulding 2008

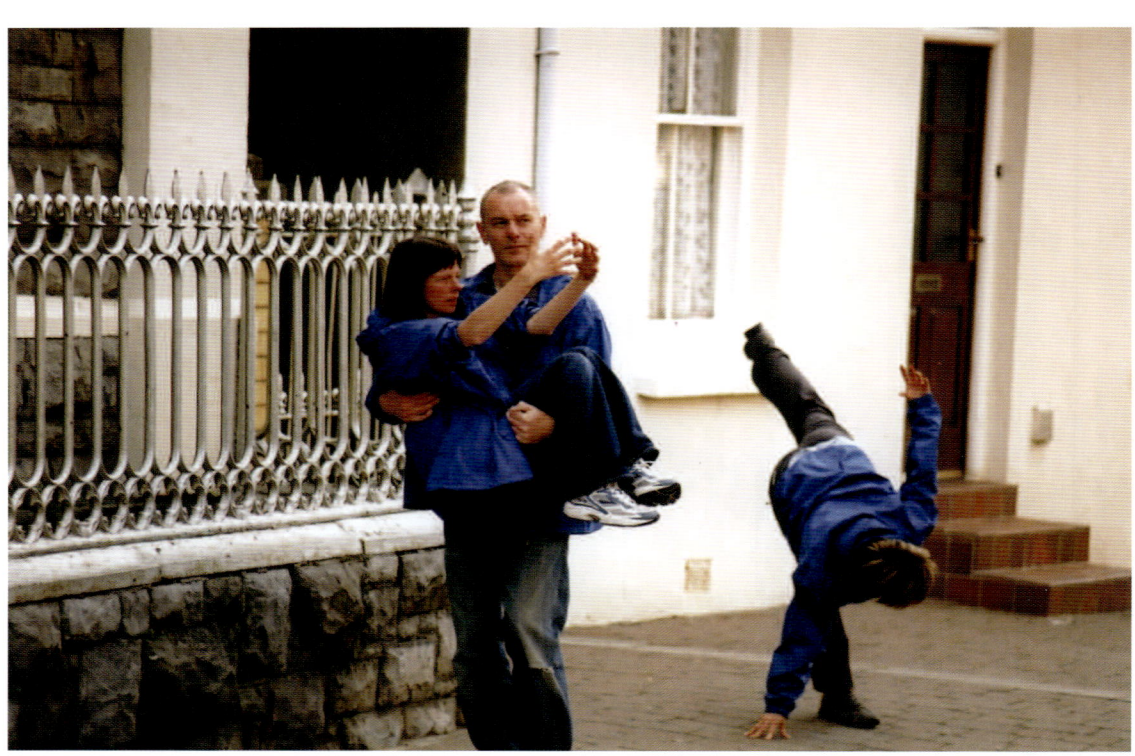

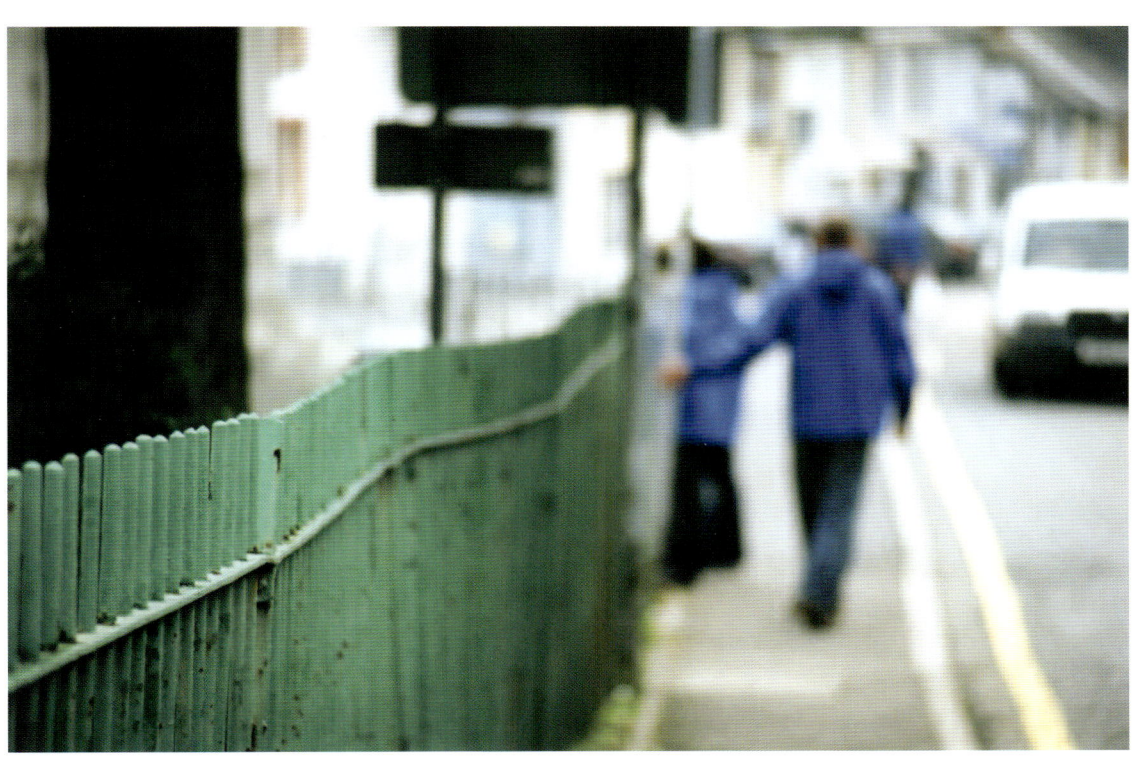

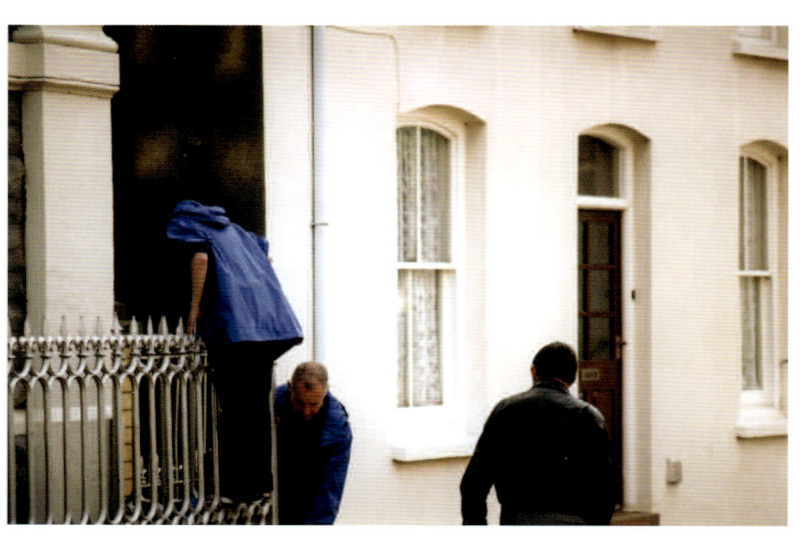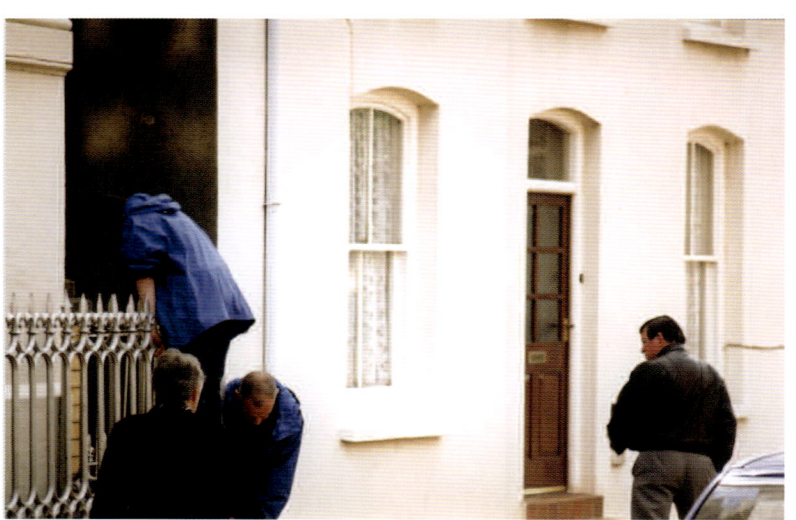

Three figures in blue cagoules began the morning *Drift* by crossing the stone bridge: Simon stood on the wall, then lay down, his arms draped to the ground. Kate and Andrea entered the scene separately, darting across the road. As they moved up towards the High Street they began to interact, though there was no sense of anyone leading or following. Behind the video camera, I was aware of passers-by trying discreetly not to notice, composing themselves as they accidentally came into shot, or apologising and ducking. The dancers moved into the streets' tucked-away spaces like the shopping arcade, where they created a spectacle for anyone who was passing: Simon shook his whole body, head raised as if in ecstatic trance. By the building site, they composed themselves as statues around the scaffolding and cement mixer. Kate stood on a wall, a temporary monument in blue nylon. A white van pulled up behind her in a side street, the driver grinning, friendly, as Simon stood with his arms outstretched as if in blessing. The dancers' movements followed the tides but they also created points of stasis, drawing the town into focus and unfolding its different layers. Andrea rolled along a wall, as if wrapping it around herself, as if she were the centre around which the town had become fluid.

The choice of blue cagoules echoed the sea, the presence of water. It also gave the dancers a slightly institutionalised air, or, rather, an air of having escaped from an institution. 'Are you *with* them?' one woman asked. I was on the other side of the road; they were carrying each other and falling. She was so genuinely concerned that I had to tell her they were dancing, though this felt like a betrayal: once given an aesthetic frame, their misbehaviour lost its capacity to send ripples of disturbance through the town. They ran on, up through the car park, and by the time I caught up with them Simon was lying on the pavement in front of a group of builders. They chuckled; the laughter faded; they asked if he was all right; he sprang up and moved on.

The journey ended at the bandstand in a small park, and it was here, late afternoon, that the afternoon drift set off in the aftermath of a heavy shower. The dancers dispersed in the dripping park: Andrea launched into a long forward roll; Kate hid and reappeared; Simon stared up at trees. Once out on the road, they stopped to chat to the builders, offering to swap jobs; there was more laughter, less anxious this time. They made their way down into town, crossing and recrossing the street. Kate crouched under a cage at a pet shop while the other two seemed to be considering either buying or rescuing her. They moved on, stopping to dance and pick dandelions in an overgrown car park, followed now by women and small children. 'Life's weird,' said a teenage boy coming the other way, sounding more resigned than surprised. A builder objected to them climbing into his skip so they ran on and down through side streets, then stopped for a while in hot sun as a car came past, distorted music blaring from its speakers. They crossed a bridge to reach a woodland path where Simon lay down, fluttering his fingers, his two-year-old daughter shrieking with delight. As they wove back into town he lay down again, this time in front of a shopkeeper locking up for the night, who said it was a nice try but he still wasn't going to open up again.

The finale was on the quay, a theatrical space glaring white into a sky that promised thunder. The dancers crawled and leaned over edges, as if growing heavy with the air. At the moment the storm broke they were away, running round and up on to the bridge, disappearing into rain.

Zoë Skoulding 2008

Ruth Jones

Inventing Rituals – Inhabiting Places

The five artists' projects for *Holy Hiatus* were commissioned by Ruth Jones in Cardigan to explore the possibilities for ritual to be employed creatively in public art practice and to examine the ways that artists can draw audiences into different, often unexpected, experiences of place through ritual. Following the completion of the projects, a series of interviews with twelve audience members were carried out by researcher Sarah Pace from Safle (an independent public art consultancy based in Cardiff) in order to gain an insight into how the artworks were received. This essay integrates the findings from these with theoretical understandings of ritual – from fields such as anthropology, sociology, cultural and communication theory – to illuminate the extent to which *Holy Hiatus* achieved its aims. The essay begins by exploring definitions of ritual and goes on to lay out the arguments for and against its creative potential. The interviewees' experiences of the artworks for *Holy Hiatus* are then compared to find support for the proposition that experiences of liminality or communitas are possible in public art projects that employ ritual. Finally, the essay looks at how experiencing public rituals in places that are familiar to us might alter our perception of those places in both exciting and challenging ways. The names of the interviewees have been altered to maintain anonymity.

Dyfeisio Defodau – Byw mewn Lleoedd

Comisiynwyd y pum prosiect gan artistiaid ar gyfer *Holy Hiatus* gan Ruth Jones yn Aberteifi er mwyn archwilio'r posibiliadau o ran defnyddio defodau'n greadigol mewn celfyddyd gyhoeddus ac archwilio'r ffyrdd y gall artistiaid dynnu cynulleidfaoedd i mewn i brofiadau gwahanol o le drwy ddefod, a hynny'n aml yn annisgwyl. Wedi cwblhau'r prosiectau, cynhaliwyd cyfres o gyfweliadau â deuddeg aelod o'r gynulleidfa gan yr ymchwilwraig Sarah Pace o Safle (ymgynghorwyr celf gyhoeddus annibynnol yng Nghaerdydd) er mwyn cael gweld beth oedd barn pobl am y gwaith celf. Mae'r erthygl hon yn plethu canfyddiadau'r cyfweliadau hyn â dealltwriaeth ddamcaniaethol o'r ddefod – o feysydd megis anthropoleg, cymdeithaseg, damcaniaethau diwylliannol a chyfathrebu – er mwyn cael gweld i ba raddau y mae *Holy Hiatus* wedi cyrraedd ei nod. Mae'r erthygl yn dechrau drwy archwilio diffiniadau o ddefod ac wedyn yn gosod y dadleuon o blaid ac yn erbyn ei photensial creadigol. Yna, mae profiadau'r rhai a gafodd eu cyf-weld o waith celf *Holy Hiatus* yn cael eu cymharu â'i gilydd er mwyn gweld a oes sail i'r awgrym bod profiadau o drothwyoledd neu *communitas* yn bosibl mewn prosiectau celf gyhoeddus sydd yn defnyddio defodau. Yn olaf, mae'r erthygl yn archwilio sut y gall profi defodau cyhoeddus mewn mannau cyfarwydd inni newid ein ffordd o feddwl am y mannau hyn mewn ffyrdd cyffrous a heriol. Mae enwau'r rhai a gafodd eu cyf-weld wedi eu newid fel y gallant barhau i fod yn anhysbys.

What Is Ritual?

The vast array of activities that come under the broad banner of 'ritual' makes definition of the term virtually impossible. Ritual is used to refer to everyday events such as mealtimes, as well as to annual celebrations and special occasions like weddings. It covers the simplest of acts, for example a handshake, through to the most structured and highly ceremonial public events such as a coronation. As Eric W. Rothenbuhler has warned, a concept designed to cover such diverse territory is 'in danger of being vacuously abstract',[1] or as Richard Schechner suggests, 'it means very little because it means too much'.[2]

There are, however, some commonly accepted qualities associated with ritual that theorists of the subject generally agree upon, the most significant of which is that ritual is understood as *action*, not simply thought, and also that it is *performed*, often marked by heightened aesthetics. There is usually something conscious and voluntary about a ritual: people are aware at some level that they are participating, an they may choose their form of participation (performer or witness) and choose the style of their participation (enthusiastic or reluctant). Rituals are not exclusively utilitarian, relating primarily to the cultural realm of ideas, symbols and aesthetics of social activity. They may be celebratory but are not just recreational; they contribute to or reinforce what anthropologist Émile Durkheim referred to as the 'serious life' and are often repetitive or have their own social rhythm. Rituals have a social or collective dimension: even when they are solitary or idiosyncratic there is always some aspect that embodies cultural codes and expresses social relations. Rituals take place in the subjunctive mood: they are often not about what *is*, but what could, might or should be.[3]

It is interesting to compare these theoretical definitions of ritual with the answers given by interviewees to the question 'Can you describe what you understand by the word ritual?' That ritual can be daily acts as well as ostentatious ceremony was acknowledged by Lowri, who described ritual as 'something as simple as preparing a meal, making a cup of tea, going to bed or getting up out of bed. Ritual pervades our lives in ways we don't even notice. Our whole lives are extremely ritualised.' At the same time, interviewees recognised that ritual was a distinctive mode of consciousness. Caroline understood ritual as 'outside your normal way of relating' and Melanie acknowledged the particular social rhythm inherent in ritual: 'It has a rhythm that lets you in and you can go back into it at that same rhythm. Repetition is an important part of ritual. You are very present in it.'

While there were many crossovers between the theoretical definitions of ritual and the interviewees' understandings of the term, what come across most powerfully in the interviews are the participants' subjective descriptions of what ritual *feels* like, the effect that it has on our being in the world. Nia describes this feeling as 'mindfulness, it's about doing the thing you're doing and not being distracted by other things'; similarly, Euan says that 'ritual enables you to clear your mind', so that it's not 'buzzing like a bunch of monkeys'; while Melanie says 'it's whole and embodied; it's about being present'. Rebecca describes this feeling as 'being in the moment and being totally present for something, whereas we spend a lot of time just in our heads not being very aware… it's about heightened attention and heightened now-ness.'

Kate emphasised the communal aspect of rituals: 'It's to do with some kind of meditation or commune with something beyond yourself or outside of yourself. Richard also refers to social engagement inherent within ritual: 'it's about relating oneself to one's environment and society and giving oneself a meaning within that society'. Rebecca believes that ritual 'should have some kind of communal aspect, but that doesn't mean that you can't carry out a ritual on your own, but… it's the universal part of doing it that brings you in touch with a greater humanity'. For Melanie this social and communal quality of ritual operates at a very deep level: 'Ritual makes room for audiences, allowing them to be present in the most profound place, inside place. It feels like magic, it's extraordinary and ordinary at the same time.' The 'magical' or transformative qualities of ritual are also emphasised by Rebecca, who describes ritual as 'something that you undertake to have some kind of transformative experience and that doesn't have to mean something grand but some kind of subtle change of experience or some kind of rite of passage'.

Creative or Conservative?

The emphasis that some of the interviewees place on the transformative nature of ritual can be seen in relation to two contested and polarized perspectives within social anthropology: the 'structural-functional' models that suggest that ritual is a tool for imposing hierarchical social and religious power; and "communitarian" models - where choice, creativity and egalitarianism are always possible in ritual action resulting from the uncertain, 'playful' and potentially transformative liminal realm. As Bobby Alexander has discussed in his essay for this book, Victor Turner was a prominent advocate of the generative potential of liminality. Other supporters of this perspective include Ronald Grimes and Clifford Geertz. It is a fascination with the creative potential of ritual that provides a primary link between the disciplines of art and anthropology and there are many well-known twentieth century examples of artists engaging with ritual: for example, Maya Deren's experimental ritual films such as *Ritual in Transfigured Time* (1946); the Ulay/Abramovic performance collaborations of the 1970s and 1980s, and Joseph Beuys' durational performances, including *I Like America and America Likes Me* (1974),

a five day performance/ritual with a coyote.

While many artists see the creative potential of ritual, not all anthropologists share this view. Key figures that have emphasised the 'structural-functional' qualities of ritual include Bronislaw Malinovski, A.R. Radcliffe-Brown and Maurice Bloch. In his essay 'Symbols, song, dance and features of articulation: is religion an extreme form of traditional authority?' Bloch uses the example of circumcision ceremonies of the Merina of Madasgar to illustrate how ceremonial speech in ritual acts is 'impoverished' and restrictive compared to day-to-day verbal exchange. He then extends his discussion to song, and then finally to dance, suggesting that there is no potential for body movements in dance that allow for bargaining, argument or discussion, these being 'replaced by fixed, repeated, fused messages'. For Bloch, to accept this code implies compulsion: 'Communication has stopped being a dialectic and has become a matter of repeating correctly.'[4] Bloch's essay is based on his research into particular ritual activities in the context of conservative tribal religious ceremonies, but from this particular situation, he makes the rather generalised conclusion that art is in fact an inferior form of communication because it disallows the generative potential of language. He accepts that this theory goes against the grain of art as a 'kind of super-communication, a supreme occasion for creativity',[5] and he seeks to find a reason why art should be believed by the majority of people to be creative:

The reason for this view probably lies in the fact that the generative processes of language are normally unconscious and that they are so complicated that they cannot be raised to a conscious level. However, when nearly all this generative potential of language (or bodily movement) has been forbidden, removed, the remaining choices left are so simple

that they can suddenly become controllable, hence enjoyable.
This, however, is an illusion of creativity; in fact this is the
sphere where it occurs least.[6]

Clearly, Bloch is not concerned in this instance with contemporary
and experimental art practices, but his ideas are relevant here because
three of the art projects for *Holy Hiatus* involved song or dance. Simon
Whitehead and his collaborators performed an improvised dance *Drift*
through the town centre, Yvonne Buchheim's swimming pool public
event involved two singers, and Maura Hazelden's performance
involved dance-like movements while her collaborator Lou Laurens
sang the thirteenth-century *Worldes Blis Ne Laste* repeatedly. While
these artists were probably using song and dance with greater freedom
than the subjects of Bloch's study, it raises the question, how do we
know when dance or song or other art forms are generative and when
they are conservative? T.J. Csordas has suggested via the work of
Stanley Tambiah on ritual language[7] that there is potential for creativity
even within a highly structured ritual through its *performativity*.
Csordas sees the fundamental difference between the methodologies
of Bloch and Tambiah as 'the perception by Bloch of a gap between a
ritual form and its "use" and the perception by Tambiah of an integral
connection between ritual form and its "performance" '.[8]

Jens Kreinath in his essay 'Ritual: theoretical issues in the study
of religion'[9] has argued that there has been a tendency for rituals to
be analysed in relation to the texts and discourses of religion. Ritual
would therefore be seen as the symbolic representation of religious
meaning. Kreinath claims that it is of vital importance that rituals
are studied and theorised on their own terms, through looking at
the actual performance of ritual action independently from religious
frameworks, uncovering how they work, in and for themselves. He
cites Clifford Geertz in suggesting that religion does not create
ritual, rituals create religions. For Geertz, this is possible because
rituals 'act to establish powerful, pervasive, and long-lasting moods
and motivations in men by formulating conceptions of a general
order of existence'.[10] Kreinath wants to explore ritual as 'a form of
human action that establishes and transforms social relations'.[11]
This perspective is most useful to understanding ritual within art
practice, since it allows for creative innovation and does not assume
that ritual is by nature authoritarian and conservative. The
interviewees from *Holy Hiatus* also predominantly identified with
this kind of definition of ritual: for example, Stuart said 'you can
create new rituals. There are historical rituals and so forth but that's
not the nature of ritual. The nature of ritual is to constantly be
reinvented, find new ritualisations, new social understandings.'

As Csordas suggests, the only way the problem of creativity in ritual
can be addressed is with an adequate theory of performance within the
context of ritual. He proposes that such a theory must pay attention to
three things: the *event* in relation to its situation and social life; the
genre, and its context within a system of genres; and the *act*. Creativity
may be found to occur at any of these levels, or in the interaction
between them. According to Csordas, it is Bloch's lack of a theory of
performance that allows him to see only constraints in ritual language,
ignoring the rhetorical skill of the performer and the dynamics of the
performer–audience relationship. Schechner recognises that 'rituals
are not safe deposit vaults of accepted ideas but in many cases dynamic
performative systems generating new materials and recombining
traditional action in new ways'.[12] He describes ritual as 'the continued
encounter between imagination and memory translated into double
acts of the body'.[13] Similarly, Csordas sees ritual language as a bodily
tool 'for reordering the behavioural environment, cultivating the
disposition of the habitus, and creating a sacred self'.[14]

So if we are to understand the creative application of ritual in relation to *Holy Hiatus* it is perhaps helpful to consider the contexts (genre, event, act) within which the art events took place. The project was advertised through brochures and in local newspapers as a series of public art events that engage with ritual, and some audience members who had read the publicity material in advance and therefore came with certain expectations were engaged actively from the outset. Many others encountered the works, particularly those by Alastair MacLennan and Simon Whitehead, spontaneously as they went about their own daily tasks. These people could choose to walk on, or to stop and engage, or even participate. For these people, it was not necessarily apparent that the events were 'art' – they were simply something unfamiliar happening in familiar places. With the partial exception of Buchheim's public event in Cardigan swimming pool, the events were not announced, nor did they make use of elaborate ceremonial trappings. However, the performances did involve simple

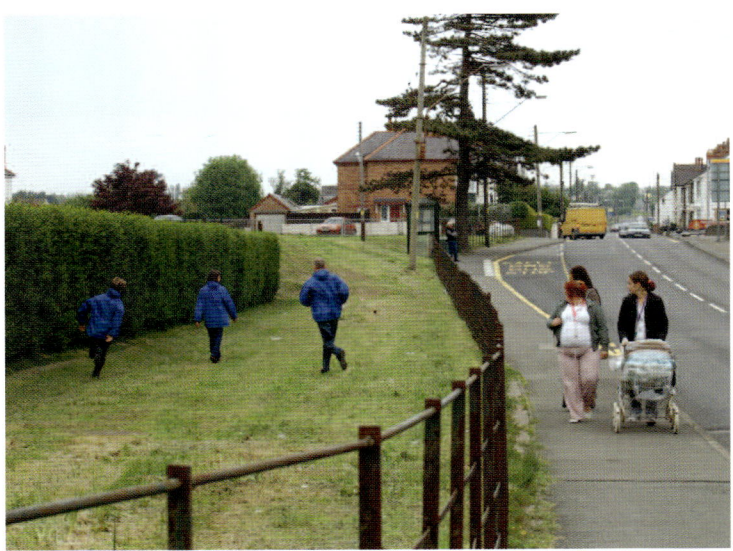

objects (MacLennan: grass, paper, ribbons, stones; Whitehead: blue anoraks; Hazelden: thyme, water, paper, pebbles). In the case of MacLennan and Whitehead, some audience members interacted spontaneously through verbal language or bodily movement.

In terms of genre and event, the projects could perhaps be identified with Turner's concept of the liminoid; that is, liminal activities carried out in western cultures that are not connected to the dominant social structures of politics or religion, but provide opportunities to let go of structural commitments, if only briefly. Liminoid activity is frequently secular, not necessarily collective or bound to calendrical or biological rhythms, and engagement is optional, not obligatory. Film, theatre and other art forms are cited as examples. Liminoid events such as these would therefore seem to allow for greater creativity, and freedom of interpretation, and therefore the question of whether each artwork employed ritual creatively can only really be approached via individual subjective responses, as what is understood by one witness/participant as liberating may be perceived by another as conservative.

From the small cross-section of audience members who were interviewed, it appears that people did understand the artworks in *Holy Hiatus* as creative of meaning. Nia describes Simon Whitehead's collaborative performance as: 'about cutting through. It was a break, a change, a flip, a new perspective on people, movement, building, the high street.' Similarly, Rebecca says: 'I liked these blue flashes going across the bridge and it was like… just like a jar across reality, or something outside breaking across, but just in a split second.' Several of the interviewees describe how the artworks made them curious or fascinated long after the events were over. After witnessing MacLennan's public performance on the footbridge, Caroline says: 'I could have talked to him about what the grass was about, for instance, Alastair, what was the grass about? And why did he dress in black? I sort of wanted to know more so I had an urge to find out more and to get to grips with what it was about.' Lynn describes how Hazelden's collaborative performance with Lou Laurens in the Small World Theatre provoked much contemplation: 'It was quite amazing. It was not until I came out that I understood about the writing that was all over the floor and I saw the translation of what the piece was about outside, which got you thinking about humanity as it is and was and what we're doing or not doing. There was a lot of thinking to be done after it.' Jackie describes how Lucas's video installation of teenagers working with animals influenced her thinking about processes: 'it's something about detail… the one with the hawk… just the way she was winding the leather strap, for instance, you know, just those bits of detail that I think are really important and I think I've overlooked things like that and sort of thought, how something is done is less important than the finished product.'

Buchheim's public event in the swimming pool clearly resonated with creative possibilities for several of the interviewees.

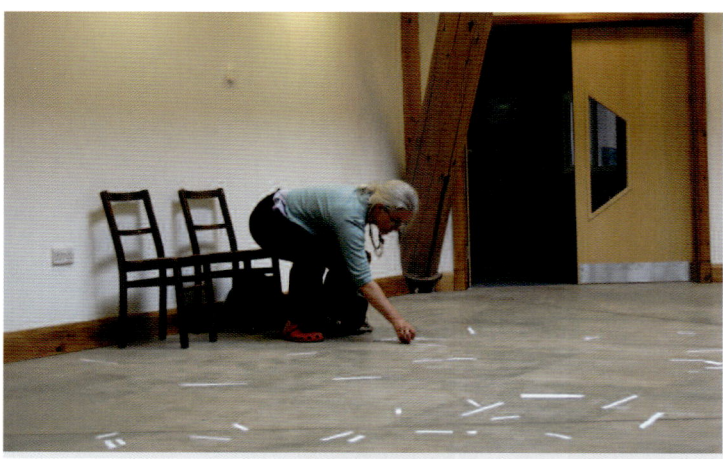

Lowri says the event 'had a sense of creating a new ritual out of an everyday ritual – in this case swimming and singing – and transforming it into something else'. Stuart elaborated on the meanings that it generated for him:

It actually made creative possibilities in the swimming pool, it played with the swimming pool potential, it played with the potential of the water, it played with the potential of the acoustic, and it did all those things and in a way it did all that on your behalf… and that was enjoyable, to see things being redrawn in that way…. You can get very deep about it and I think there's resonances with birth and rebirth… it was as though the singers were celebrants, there were these non-participant individuals who just sat in these big bubbles but a different, a very different relationship with the water – they were on the water but not in the water, whereas the two swimmers were in the water all the time and that made you speculate about being part of something and not part of something.

While the interviewees clearly enjoyed exploring possible meanings generated by the art events for *Holy Hiatus*, they also acknowledged that in some circumstances, structured ritual plays an important role. Stuart, who was about to undertake jury service, discussed how different that situation was to an art project: 'part of the ritualisation of a courtroom has to indicate what the rights of people are and the limits of the process… I mean swearing on the bible or whatever you have to do… all of that has got a practical purpose… otherwise the system wouldn't work, would it?' Kate points out that 'human beings need rituals; they are fundamental to our lives because we need to have security about our being in the world', while Nia described how

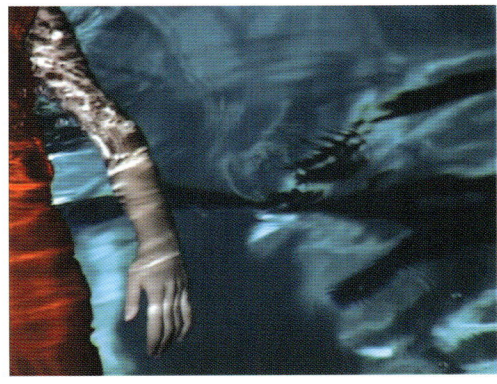 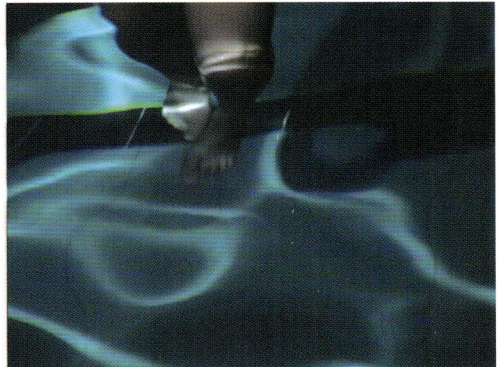 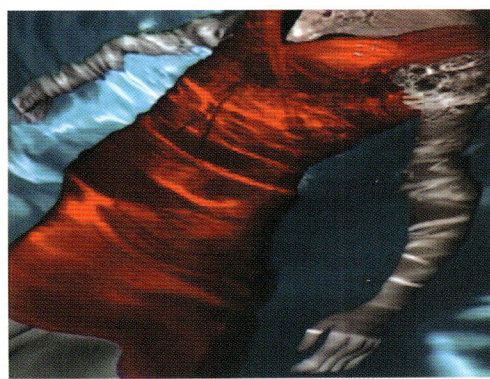

when she was affected by periods of depression, simple day-to-day activities performed with attention such as laying the table were 'a method of clearing the fog and making a structure'. She adds: 'its all rather big, life's rather big and you sometimes need certain things that you can anchor onto'. Like many binaries, the polarity between structure and anti-structure, or liminality, is often unhelpful. The presence of structure does not deny creativity, in fact all action requires some degree of structure to be able to manifest. Perhaps the question posed should be not is the artwork creative or conservative, but how does it influence our perception of our relationships with others, with our wider environment, with place, and community, and how does this empower future action or thought in positive, inclusive and expansive ways? Schechner describes how the future of ritual lies in striking a balance between structure and anti-structure: 'Ritual's conservatism may restrain humans enough to prevent our extinction, while its magmatic creative core demands that human life – social, individual, maybe even biological – keeps changing.'[15]

Wholly Attending – Liminality in Public Art
One of the aims of *Holy Hiatus* was to explore whether it was possible

for artists to employ ritual to draw audiences into different states of consciousness, to experience liminality or even Turner's *communitas*, which is distinct from liminality in that it is always shared by at least two people, while liminal experience can be solitary. Why is it important to experience liminality? And why might art be an appropriate vehicle for this? Turner perceived that ritual is in decline in modern societies, having shifted from a collective, often obligatory activity to fragmented practices on the periphery of the social process.[16] As Alexander has illustrated in his book *Victor Turner Revisited: Ritual as Social Change*, Turner proposes that ritual is a response to the division, alienation and exploitation that are associated with everyday social structure. By suspending these structures, ritual may create direct and egalitarian exchanges and invite experimentation with alternative communitarian relations. Ritual is associated with the subjunctive mood, a realm of pure possibility in which experiences generated *could* introduce innovations into the social structure.

Turner uses the term 'communitas' to refer to 'a quality of human interrelatedness that can "emerge" from or "descend" upon two or more human beings'[17] during the liminal phase of a ritual action. Communitas unmasks the arbitrary distinctions inherent to social structure and allows humans to interact with one another, 'not as role players but as "human totals", integral beings who share the same humanity'.[18] It also represents 'the desire for a total unmediated relationship between person and person… in the very act of realising their commonness'.[19] It is not an expression of a type of herd instinct, but of humans 'in their wholeness wholly attending'.[20] Turner does not deny the need for structure within society, but suggests that our need for communitas is just as great.

It is also possible that rituals have a beneficial biological effect. Within the fields of psychology, neurology and biogenetics, research suggests that the 'oceanic' feeling of belonging, ecstasy and total participation that many people experience during rituals works by means of repetitive rhythms, sounds and tones that 'tune' the left and right hemispheres of the cerebral cortex to one another.[21] Individual and collective anxieties are relieved by the rhythmic qualities of rituals, stimulating the brain into releasing endorphins into the bloodstream, inducing pleasure and relieving pain.[22] Some researchers suggest that rather than fulfilling a purely cultural need, the desire to ritualise is hardwired into the human brain. Barbara Ehrenreich in her book *Dancing in the Streets: A History of Collective Joy* speculates that group rituals involving dance may have evolved as a means to create a common emotional bond between people within human communities that were growing in size during the Palaeolithic period, thus making the group more effective at defending themselves from predators and achieving other common aims.[23]

Holy Hiatus brought together a number of artists who had employed ritual in previous projects to make new works in Cardigan that responded to the themes of ritual, place and community. In the act of making the works, the effect that these would have for audiences was unknown, although it was hoped that something akin to liminality or communitas would be accessible for some people some of the time. Turning to the interviewees' answers to the question 'Can you describe what you felt during the artworks?' some interesting responses emerged.[24] Alastair MacLennan's twelve-hour 'actuation' on the footbridge that crosses the River Teifi generated significant interest. This ranged from simple curiosity to meaningful encounters such as Melanie's:

> As we approached the bridge we saw a man in a black hat doing something with purpose and rhythm, which was calming, and we saw the white ribbons on the bridge. By the time we reached him, I felt calmer. I was surprised because he looked up and said 'hello', but without shifting from what he was doing, which made you feel part of it. It was like watching someone knitting or sewing, the rhythm and repetition draws you in; it separates you from your head and you're in the rhythm. Like when you listen to music and you're in the melody. It was a very profound place to be – in his ritual.

While Melanie understood Alastair's performance as 'his' ritual, she still felt drawn into it. Other interviewees felt that more direct participation in a ritual would be necessary to create an inclusive experience. Lowri says 'I'm not sure how successfully [the artworks] could create liminal experiences for people who were not integrally involved in the ritual.' Rebecca illustrates this when she discusses her experience of Buchheim's event. She saw the setting as 'theatrical… it's happening and you're experiencing it but you're not quite involved in it'. She describes how at the end of the performance, she 'had this real urge… to be in the water, I wanted to be swimming and be involved in it. At the end I just went and

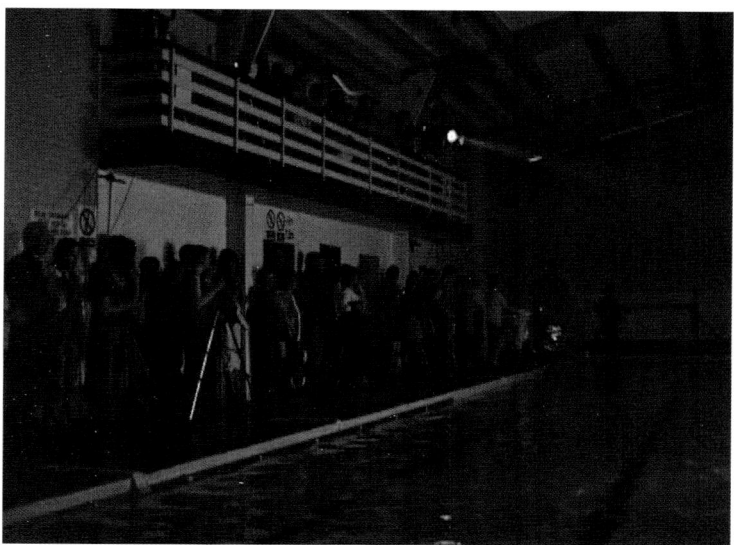

communitas had taken place at the pool, at least for some of those present. This is supported by Melanie's experience:

There was a rhythm and a sense of being in the ritual, repeated through the movement of the swimmers… it was a very complete and satisfying experience that was sad in moments. Like the girl in the red dress trying to get away…

It brought the audience on a risky journey but it offered a known space that created trust and let us in, allowing us to delve into liminal space. It was sublime.… The first time around the words really bothered me; I thought the lyrics were too literal. I thought 'don't tell me what to experience', but then… I got into the chant. The heat was great and the thunder and the rain. People were hushed and shuffling in to see it.

put my hand in the water, I wanted to know what the experience was because it felt like the people doing it were doing the ritual, it was an impulse to join it.' She felt that the work was framed in such a way that spontaneous interaction was not invited: 'It was a very specific image being created and that wasn't to be disrupted.' Richard felt that 'the nature of spectacle took over' for him in this event. He says: 'I didn't connect with it… I felt crowded and there was so much going on… it felt difficult to focus and for it all to come together into one experience.'

In contrast, Stuart felt moved by the event at the pool and believed that others there had felt the same way: 'On the way out there was that genuine sense of having shared an experience, I'm not sure everyone would feel the same, but going out, there was eye contact with people and a sense of having been part of something.' This comment would suggest that something akin to Turner's

Maura Hazelden's performance, which took place over a six-hour period, provoked powerful responses. Some of the interviewees equated it to a religious or spiritual experience, heightened by the expansive and vault-like space of the newly built Small World Theatre lit by the evening sun. Lynn said 'It felt like a sort of cathedral. It was a very spiritual, prayerful experience. The voice was so haunting; like a lament.' Richard described the work as having 'a very quiet understated presence in Cardigan, but it had a lot of impact. It was a very calm, thoughtful, meditative piece, which demanded a lot of time.' Euan, who regularly takes part in group meditation, describes how he was quickly drawn into a contemplative space, perhaps akin to the liminal:

Well, it affected me because it was the first time we'd been in that particular theatre… and then when Maura started, I was

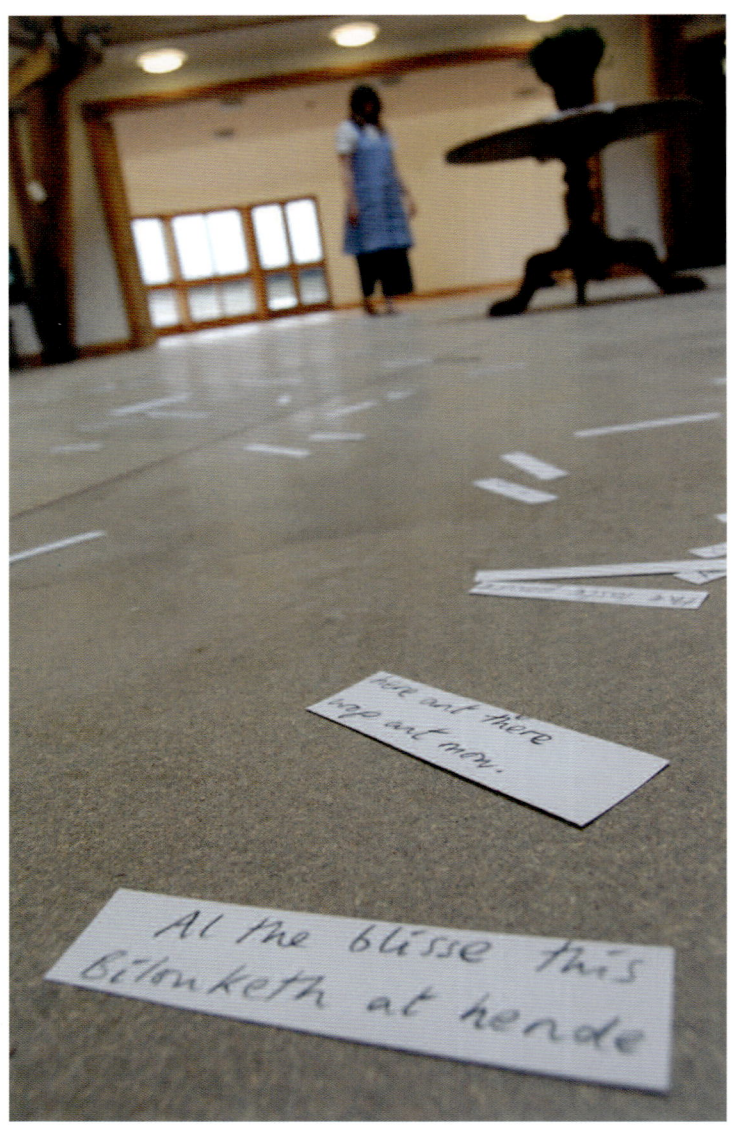

fascinated by simply watching her feet, although she used the whole of her body, I just focused on that... we simply sat, completely silent, and it was as though we were meditating, and the mantra was her movements.

Rebecca described how the performance stimulated all of the senses, contributing to a whole experience that was profoundly affecting:

Before we went in we were told to pick up a stone so you immediately had a focus of your attention and it was very minimalist, but there was also a lot to look at because the [space] was strewn with bits of paper and Maura was doing her movement score. And the impulse was just to sit down and stay in one place with it. And it was a meditative thing. The way the singing cut in and out was very effective, very simple. There was smell as well, it was like all your attentions were given some kind of focus... they'd rubbed thyme on the stone, and I was putting it on my face and so I was getting the smell, quite quickly it drew you into a contemplative space, but there was also enough dynamic and change to keep you with it as well.

With both Buchheim's event at the pool and Hazelden's performance in a theatre space, the distinction between the collective catharsis of theatre and participation in a ritual became blurred, with some attendees perceiving themselves as observers and others as participants. Although there was no obvious invitation to actively participate in Hazelden's performance, Euan and Rebecca felt drawn into the presence of the event. Other interviewees perceived a more definite distinction between performer and audience. Although Richard described the event as 'very moving', he felt that his role was as an observer rather than a participant, and that the venue as a theatre had 'a number of connotations' that meant that he did not 'cross the line between audience member and performer'. Mary, who was interviewed at the same time as Euan, felt very aware of the intensity of Maura's focused attention, but she did not feel that she participated in the event:

> As we left… we looked back through one of the windows and saw Maura there and I found that very effecting, to see her through the glass in a space on her own. And on reflection… I felt that we were intruding on her. I know the idea was that we should partake, but I think what I felt was that it was such a personal thing to her that we were almost superfluous to her requirements, she didn't need an audience to do it… she would have done it anyway.

Euan responded to this with: 'I just felt I was part of it and that I wasn't intruding on Maura and we were part of the same thing. It's like, for example, you can do yoga by yourself or you can do it in a group.' For Caroline, the repetitive nature of the performance broke through the traditional linear theatre experience because she 'wasn't trying to grab the experience like you might do when you go to the theatre where it's important that you take the whole thing in'. She describes how although there was movement and singing, these contributed to a sense of restfulness: 'It did affect me afterwards. I felt still and quiet within myself for a length of time and reflective about stillness because there's not a lot of stillness currently in the world and I kind of crave it. It was very moving.' Caroline describes the process through which, for her, witnessing became an increasingly participatory act as time went by:

> Maura was just sort of there doing these strange movements, going through this process of her own. So you're sort of witnessing her journey in some way, but still reverent in that… it was like seeing something very beautiful or like experiencing nature in a way, a kind of quietness came over you and you sort of took it in, the same reverence you might have for a kind of quality of really paying attention.

Place, Community and Ritual

Questions surrounding participation and non-participation that came to the fore in the interviews are highly significant for art projects that take place within the public domain. While galleries can give artists a *carte-blanche* to reinvent space imaginatively, without necessarily addressing the particularities of place or community, public art projects tread a much finer line between the aims of the artist and the perceptions of those intimately connected with a place, sometimes encountering quite vociferous public criticism. This has been illustrated in Cardigan following its successful bid to commission a new piece of semi-permanent public art as part of Channel 4's Big Art Project. Intense public discussions have taken place between the project's supporters, who believe that the interactive floating installation on the Teifi by Rafael Lozano-Hemmer will encourage public participation and enhance the newly built Prince Charles Quay, promote tourism and help to develop the growing arts profile of Cardigan, and its detractors, who are concerned about possible environmental impacts, the potential for vandalism and decay of the work, and question the sums of money at stake to achieve its realisation. *Holy Hiatus* took place in the midst of these debates, and it was far from clear at the outset what kind of public reactions would ensue.

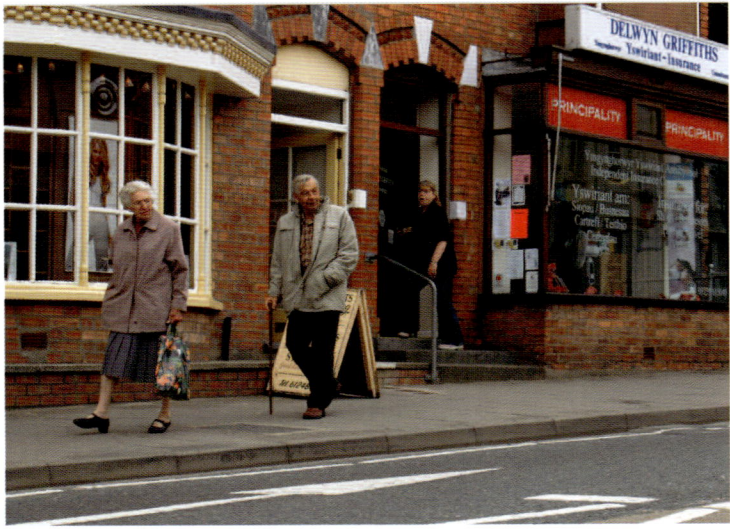

The temporary nature of the *Holy Hiatus* events, their relatively low budgets and the 'playfulness' that characterised many of the artworks worked to their advantage in this context. The events left no physical traces, but nonetheless created a buzz of interest that lived on in people's memories. Ben Stammers, who was invited by Whitehead to follow the dancers and respond to *Drift* with still images, describes how, having lost sight of the performers, he tried to relocate them by asking people if they had seen three people in blue raincoats, and it became clear that the dancers' activities were prompting spontaneous interactions between curious townspeople:

Nearly everyone I asked had seen the blue coats, or had heard about them – a smile mostly came to the face in response to my question, usually with a raised eyebrow, and they nearly all had questions for me in return – what was it all about? Was I one of them?

Talking to a lady stood in a shop doorway (in English), a group of three people on the main street (in Welsh) and a group of cockney builders not only allowed me to pick up the trail and eventually catch up with the dancers, but also gave me a real sense of the trace they had left through the town – an undocumented effect that is now left in the perceptions and conversations of the people that glimpsed them or heard about them.

For some of the interviewees, particular works prompted creative shifts in their thinking about familiar places, Richard says: 'now that I've seen Simon's piece, whenever I walk up and down the High Street in Cardigan, I've got that in mind… I'm just much more aware of moving around the town, I think, but always with him in mind. It's quite humorous, the more I think about it now.' About Buchheim's event in the swimming pool, Stuart says: 'there was that evocation of a local pool being a place where all sorts might happen, of a spiritual nature and other kinds of things, baptisms and what-have-you… that was an interesting redrawing of the space for me'.

The reciprocal exchange of ideas between artists and audiences or participants is a quality of 'dialogical' public art that Grant Kester promotes in his book *Conversation Pieces*. The facilitation of dialogue (verbal or non-verbal) in public art can 'help us speak and imagine beyond the limits of fixed identities, official discourse, and the perceived inevitability of partisan political conflict', allowing the art project to 'unfold through a process of performative interaction'.[25] This process-based approach has the potential for viewers' responses to affect the evolution of the artwork and challenges assumptions about the relationships between art, artist, audiences and the wider social and political environment. While it is not strictly speaking an art 'movement', the dialogical approach has characterised some aspects of community orientated and temporary public art since the 1960s, following a growing dissatisfaction with the cultural division of art-spaces and life-spaces. The softening of these boundaries is timely for contemporary practices that explore ritual in public spaces, such as those commissioned for *Holy Hiatus*, since possibilities arise for interaction with ritual activity that is perhaps lacking in other areas of people's lives. Stuart confirms this when he says: 'there is a gap in my life as far as ritual is concerned and I'd probably like to be able to involve myself more'. Lowri also perceived a contemporary diminishment of shared ritual experiences: 'there is a lack of rituals that engage all levels of the community, such as going to chapel did, say a hundred years ago, when people shared an experience together no matter what age they were or how different they were in their daily lives'.

Some interviewees who lived in Cardigan felt concerned that audiences who did not have prior knowledge of the *Holy Hiatus* events, or perhaps had little or no experience of this kind of art practice, might feel alienated by the works. Rebecca felt that 'a ritual needs participation and the people involved in that actually need to know what it is and how they are participating and that's what you don't have if it's an art event, you don't actually know what the rules are like you do with a religious ritual or another social kind of ritual'. It is true that while much temporary public art practice contains an implicit invitation to participate, some people will have the 'cultural capital' to understand this and take up the invitation, while others may not. Similarly, Lowri expressed concern that 'a ritual in which you don't know how to behave, like some of the artworks in *Holy Hiatus*, may be alienating and people may not have attended them for fear of

not knowing how to behave'. Despite this unease, Lowri describes how Whitehead's dance *Drift* 'felt like a joint piece with the town's people'. She says that 'everyone was a participant; the bystanders

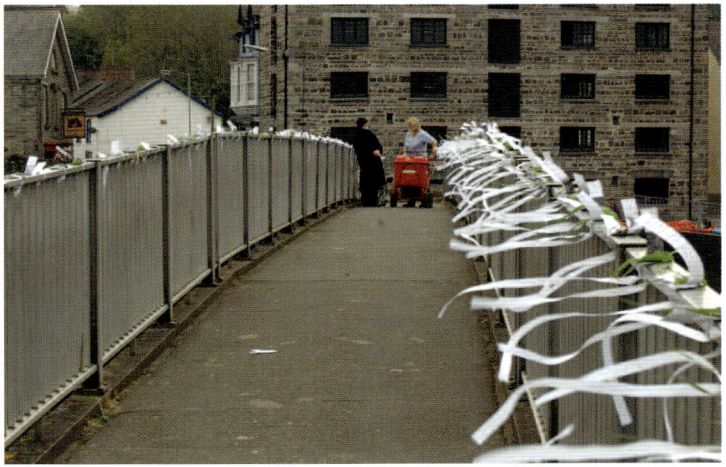

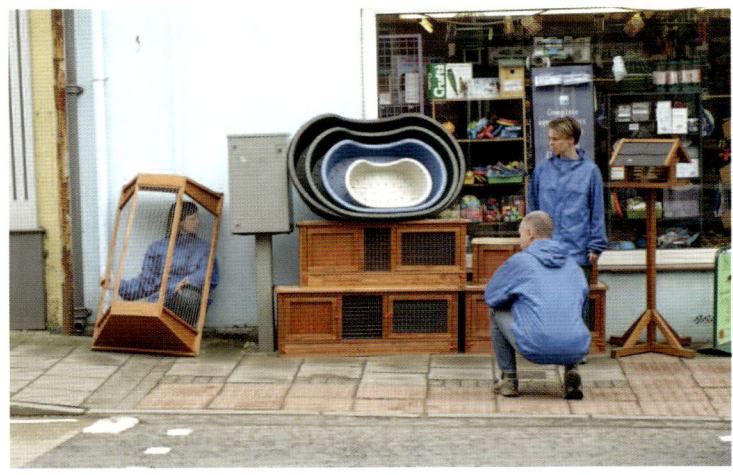

were in full view during the piece and so formed part of it'.

Nia also felt that Whitehead's event was interactive and it was clear that something out of the ordinary was happening: 'I think that even if you hadn't been expecting them that you might have noticed that there was something jaunty about the way they were walking.' She describes how she stayed in one position and observed the dancers 'getting physical with the signposts'. She found the experience really enjoyable and felt that 'they did seem to interact with the public. I can remember seeing one bit when someone walked past them and that seemed to trigger them to carry on, to move further… there was a certain playfulness that was going on amongst them and yet serious as well.' Perhaps the person that Nia saw was Melanie, who describes how she chose to participate more actively: 'I watched other people ignoring them, and so I decided to set myself a challenge. I walked past them very fast and went around the corner to see how they would respond. When I moved past them, they moved faster. It was very playful.'

Caroline felt that Hazelden's performance invited multi-layered interpretation and was interactive with the audience: 'I think there was quite a lot of space in a way to have your feelings and because it was in a building that was enclosed, it was quite private. [Lou] said I looked really serious and she felt that her song was getting quieter and quieter in response to me, which was really interesting because I didn't think she could see me… so it was interactive partly, I was sort of serious and she had to change her song in relation to who was in the room.' Similarly, Richard felt that MacLennan's twelve-hour performance on the footbridge had a celebratory feel that was also participatory, and this had a lot to do with MacLennan's gentle pace and open body language, which invited interaction, but did not force it upon the passers-by:

Alastair's was so firmly rooted in the community and in a public space that people couldn't avoid, people had to walk across the bridge to get into Cardigan… you had to experience this thing and you could either bypass it, or you can even talk to him about it, it was very much there and participative… it was temporary, very subtle and jubilant within Cardigan that kind of lifted people a bit and drew attention to the water and to the surrounding area. I thought it worked really well from that point of view… [he was] just being there and doing his thing, he was putting up no barriers, it was 'here I am, I'm doing my thing and come and talk to me about it, we can have a great long chat, I'm here all day.'

Caroline also describes how MacLennan's performance in a calm and understated way focused public attention on the footbridge. Normally a functional transitional non-place between Cardigan and St Dogmaels, the bridge was made strange by the activity occurring on it: 'I felt excited by that, I felt that I was participating in this strange event, that we all were, but in a very low-key way.'

For some of the interviewees who lived in and around Cardigan, the artworks resonated deeply because of their close connection to the town. Nia explained that this was 'one of the reasons I was quite excited about the project… it was a very personal thing to see something happen in my own town that was of interest'. She describes how she saw people interacting with MacLennan on the bridge and that this experience stayed with her even when she could no longer see him: 'I enjoyed it being there and enjoyed knowing it was there even when I wasn't there and that's because of my relationship to the town.' The relationship between place and ritual is paradoxical. The particularity of place can be a primary stimulus to the development of a ritual, but on the other hand, Turner talks about ritual liminality as 'a place that is not a place'. Is ritual about transporting oneself 'out of place', to another kind of consciousness, or about gaining a deeper understanding of and relationship to a place? Grimes suggests that perhaps it can be both:

Ritualists dance… to discover ways of inhabiting a place… ritual helps people figure out, divine, even construct a cosmos. A cosmos is not merely an empty everywhere, it is an everywhere as perceived from somewhere, a universe as construed from a locale. A cosmos is a topocosm, a universe in this place, an oriented, 'cosmosized' place, a this-place which is also an every-where.[26]

Rebecca describes how experiencing both MacLennan's actuation and the culmination of Whitehead's *Drift* on the bridge in relation to other ritual activities occurring in the town at the same time brought her in touch simultaneously with her familiar hometown and with more universal human experiences, in this case death:

When I was down on the quayside… it was about to really pour with rain so I went into the Grovenor Pub to shelter and there were people in there. I think there'd been a funeral, well, there were people dressed in black ties so I presumed that was what was going on and that experience was as much part of whatever was going on outside, so to be in that pub with people and sheltering from the rain and a bit of interaction with people coming through the door and you were part of something… there it was in front of your eyes and I'll remember that with fondness… I suppose because I'm from Cardigan as well so what I liked was going somewhere really familiar and there was something strange happening on the bridge… some public art happening but everybody was sheltering in this pub, looking through the door… and somebody had died, but there we were.

In his chapter on 'Ritual in Environmental Space' in *Rite out of Place*, Grimes poses a tongue-in-cheek question not normally raised by conventional ritual theory: 'Is ritualizing good for the planet?' He calls for greater specificity within our understanding of ritual action, suggesting that certain kinds of ritual practices may aid our evolution through enhancing adaptability, but adds that highly structured and rigid ritualised human life can encourage one-dimensional, stereotyped and inflexible identities. Loss of gestural diversity would be damaging to human evolution, so it is important for us to be discriminating about the kinds of rituals in which we partake and those which we choose to forgo. *Holy Hiatus* engaged directly with many big questions about ritual in order to contribute to a process of greater discernment about the nature of contemporary ritual activity, and the role that art can play in this process. It is hoped that the events and their contextualisation within this book will prompt further exploration into the potential value of ritual to human community and identity.

Maura Hazelden

Untitled

Performance in collaboration with Lou Laurens

A phrase of movement and a thirteenth-century song,
Worldes Blis Ne Laste, repeated over 6 hours.

The Small World Theatre, Cardigan
4–6.45 p.m. and 7.15 –10.30 p.m.
Thursday 22nd May 2008

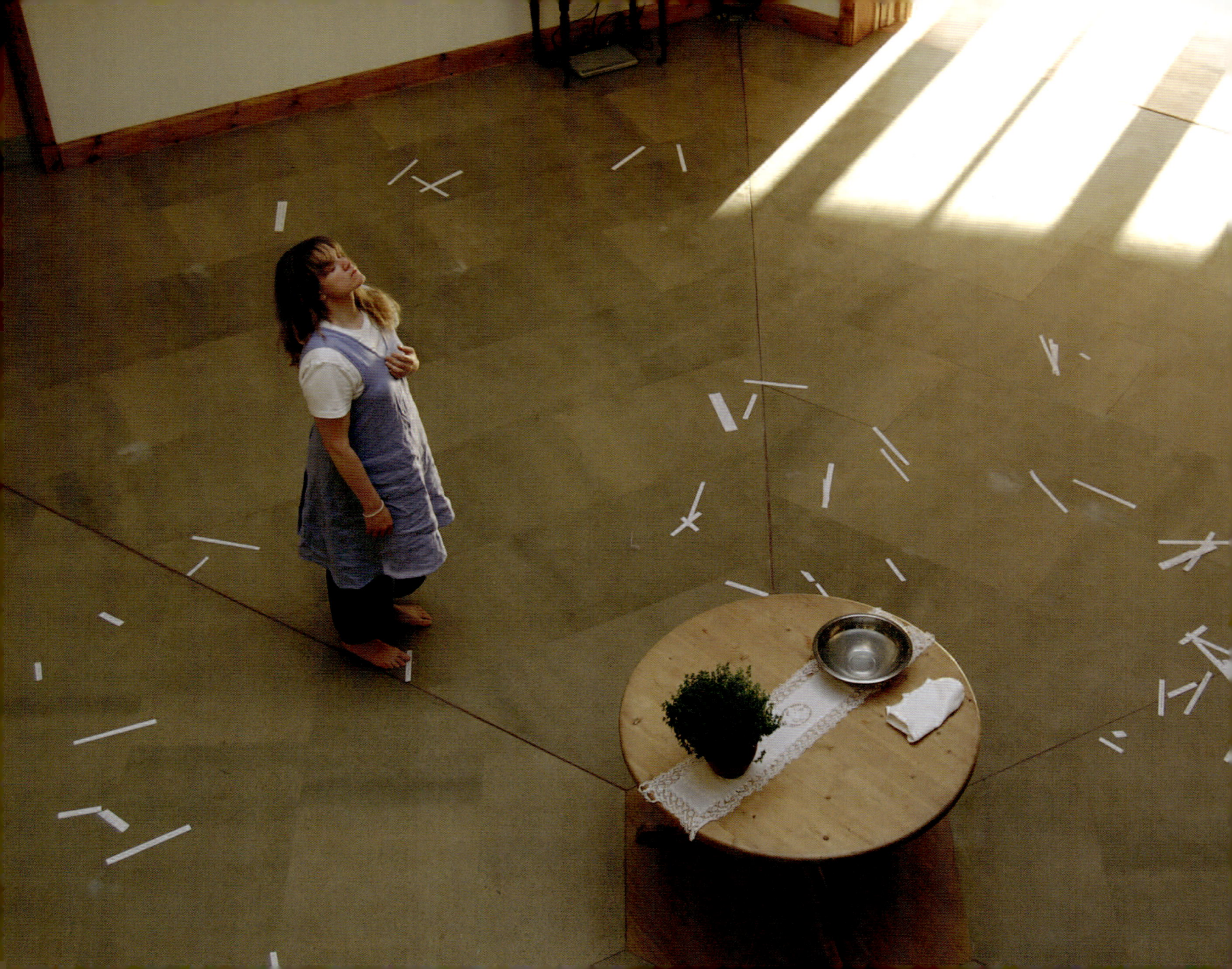

1. Standing by the corner outside the Canteen cafe in Newport, about six o'clock.

'You must talk to me about your performance.'
Arm stretch up to pale half-moon overhead.
'I think I have the first movement.'

2 . Table/land from above

'As a memory it all seems like a grainy photograph, I float into a stream moving slowly in my head, I stretch into a beech tree with both sound and vision.'

3. (on Sunday 10th May) Pale new moon outside the cottage:

'I think I have the second movement. STARS in your eyes!'

FIRST FOOTING –
RITUAL DANCE

left right – turn
and exhultation –
a foot – feet
between body
& floor
where are
the hands –
while feet are
bound
in leather
on the floor

concentrate on the
walking.

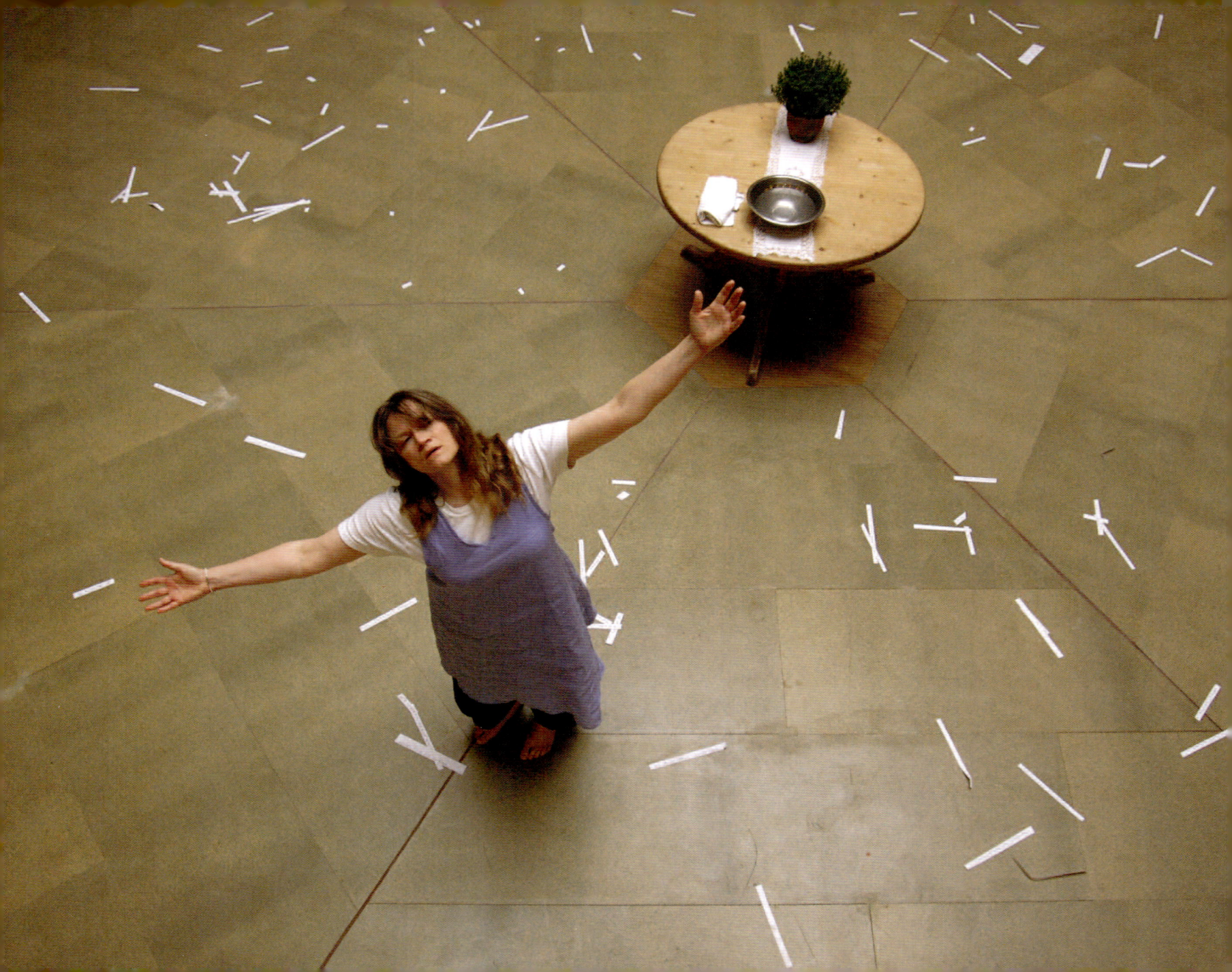

Singing
from above –
harmonium
sets off
yet another
repeat of an old
English song –
floor
covered with
strips
of paper
of that song

foot scuffles
from a deep
distant past

The question of
being someone's
amanuensis
(copywriter)
but not as
storyteller
more
a silent
encounter
between
body
and floor –

how to record off
the sleeve or (off)
the cuff

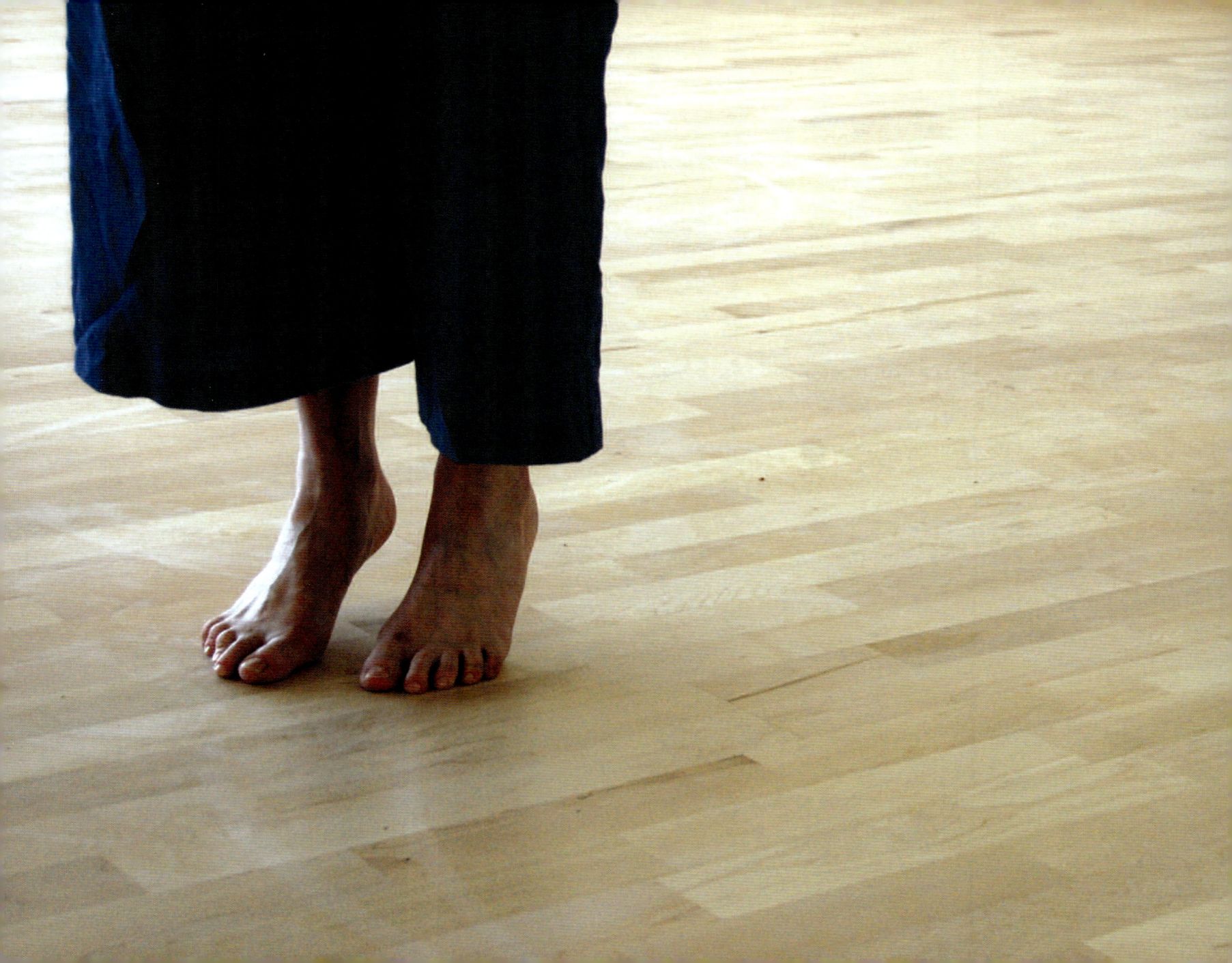

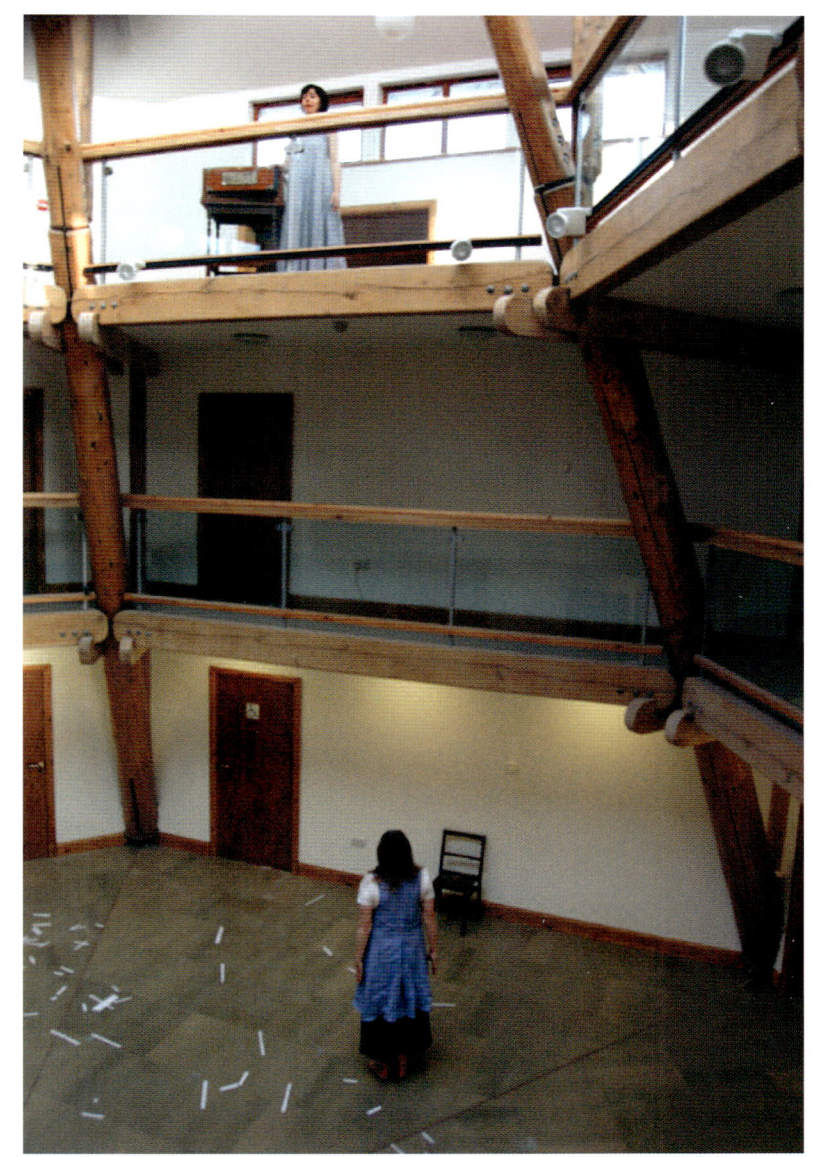

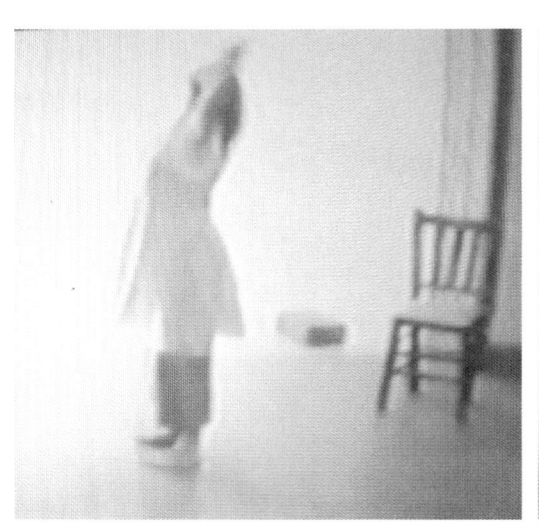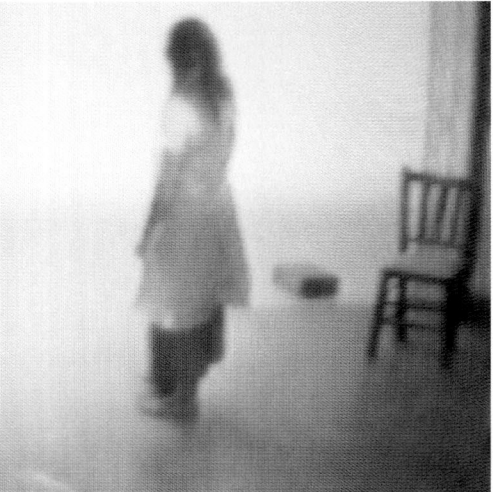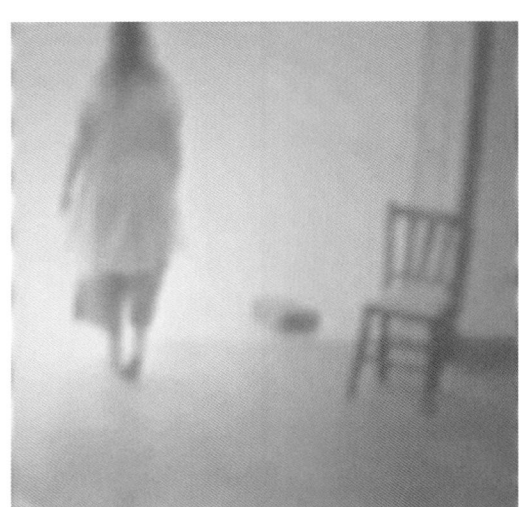

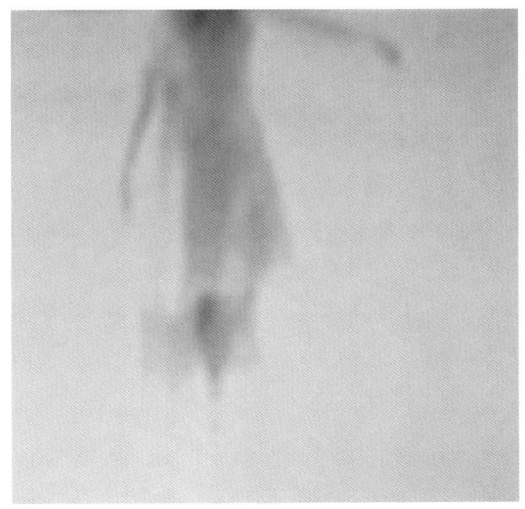

Ambage: round about, windings, circuitous route – dark & mysterious courses.

Ambient : going around – an encompassing sphere.

Amanuenses: recalling (of things past) to memory – as distant as a history of illness given by a patient to a physician

An edited response to the performance and process
John Sharkey 2009

Samantha Hurn

Humans and Other Animals in the Work of Anna Lucas: A Conversation with the Artist

Anna Lucas was one of the five artists commissioned to make a new piece of work for *Holy Hiatus* that responded to the themes of ritual, place and community. Lucas's previous video installations such as *Paloma Ceffyl* 2005 and *Lamps and Lurchers* 2003 indicated an interest in the complex interactions between humans, animals and the environments that they inhabit. Lucas undertook a three-week residency in West Wales to research and gather 16mm film footage for a new installation that would document the relationships between teenagers and working animals in this area. The resulting film, *Begail Foxwell Whip*, was installed in the Pendre Art Gallery and café in Cardigan. During the research and development of this project, Lucas came into contact with Dr Samantha Hurn, a lecturer in Social Anthropology at the University of Wales in Lampeter, specializing in anthrozoology or the comparative study of human interactions with non-human animals in a wide range of cultural contexts. Her research interests include the different ways in which humans and non-human animals perceive and engage with their environments and each other, and the various forms of indirect, inter-species communication which occur during these interactions, with particular reference to farming, hunting and outdoor leisure pursuits. The connections between Hurn's research and Lucas's practice invited further investigation, and an informal conversation between them took place at the symposium for *Holy Hiatus*. An edited transcript from this discussion is presented, together with images of relevant works by Lucas.

Bodau Dynol ac Anifeiliaid Eraill yng Ngwaith Anna Lucas: Sgwrs â'r Artist

Anna Lucas yw un o'r pum artist a gomisiynwyd i wneud darn o waith newydd ar gyfer *Holy Hiatus* a oedd yn ymateb i themâu defod, lle a chymuned. Mae gosodiadau fideo blaenorol Lucas megis *Paloma Ceffyl* 2005 a *Lamps and Lurchers* 2003 yn dangos ei diddordeb yn y berthynas gymhleth rhwng bodau dynol, anifeiliaid, a'r amgylcheddau y maent yn byw ynddynt. Treuliodd Lucas dair wythnos yng Ngorllewin Cymru er mwyn gwneud gwaith ymchwil a chasglu deunydd ffilm 16 mm ar gyfer gosodiad newydd a fyddai'n cofnodi'r berthynas rhwng pobl ifanc yn eu harddegau ac anifeiliaid gwaith yn yr ardal hon. Cafodd y ffilm, *Begail Foxwell Whip*, ei gosod yn Oriel Gelf a chaffi Pendre yn Aberteifi. Yn ystod y gwaith ymchwil a datblygu i'r prosiect hwn, daeth Lucas ar draws y Dr Samantha Hurn, darlithydd mewn Anthropoleg Gymdeithasol ym Mhrifysgol Cymru Llanbedr Pont Steffan, sydd yn arbenigo mewn Anthroswoleg neu astudiaeth gymharol o ryngweithio'r ddynolryw ag anifeiliaid mewn sawl cyd-destun diwylliannol. Mae ei meysydd ymchwil yn cynnwys y gwahanol ffyrdd y mae bodau dynol ac anifeiliaid yn gweld eu hamgylchedd ac yn ymwneud ag ef a chyda'i gilydd, a'r amryw ffyrdd o gyfathrebu anuniongyrchol, rhyng-rywogaethol sydd yn digwydd yn ystod y rhyngweithio hwn, yn enwedig yng nghyd-destun ffermio, hela a gweithgareddau awyr agored. Yr oedd y cysylltiadau rhwng ymchwil Hurn ac ymarfer Lucas yn gofyn am ragor o ymchwil, a chafwyd sgwrs anffurfiol rhyngddynt yn symposiwm *Holy Hiatus*. Cyflwynir trawsgrifiad o'r drafodaeth hon wedi ei olygu, ynghyd â delweddau o weithiau perthnasol gan Lucas.

(Before conversation starts, Anna shows *Paloma Ceffyl*: a film of a woman massaging a horse)

Sam: I thought I'd start off by introducing myself and explaining why, as an anthropologist, I'm particularly interested in Anna's work. I also wanted to reiterate that this is going to be quite a fluid, informal conversation because I haven't actually seen all of the pieces Anna is showing here before, so a lot of this is new to me as well.

I'm a lecturer in Anthropology at the University of Wales in Lampeter, and I was particularly excited when Ruth invited me to discuss Anna's work with her here today because my own research interests incorporate many of the central themes, not only of Anna's work, but also of this symposium in general. I am primarily concerned with the many and varied ways in which humans engage with non-human animals, specifically in ritual contexts. My own doctoral research was conducted locally, living and working as a member of the farming community, and the main focus was the local mounted foxhunt. I spent a total of eight years looking at the way that farmers engage with animals and the local environment and as a result of that period of participant observation, I've also become interested in the importance of horses to the local farming economy, and the way that humans think about horses – how they interact with them, and the way non-human animals can become extensions of the human self – and so I was particularly interested in this piece. So maybe if Anna just gives a bit of context about the film, and then perhaps I can elaborate further on the human–horse bond from an anthropological perspective.

Anna: I showed that piece because it began with a New Year's Eve at a farm nearby, where I was sitting with two friends, one of who grew up very near to here. We were all doing those drawings of 'what do you want in the next year, and if you draw it you're going to get it'. I had a feeling that I had not had any interaction with animals for a really long time, I was living in London – I had no cat even. So I'd drawn a picture of myself on a horse, and when we all looked at our drawings, it turned out the other two had also drawn pictures of themselves on horses, so we started talking about why. It transpired that Barley, who's the woman shown in this film, had taught herself to ride and had always had the Preseli hills in her view but had never managed to reach them, because she lived just too far to get to them

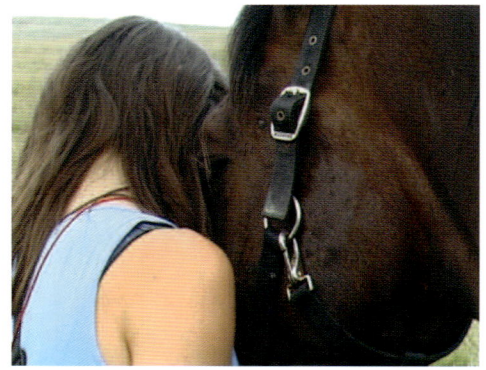
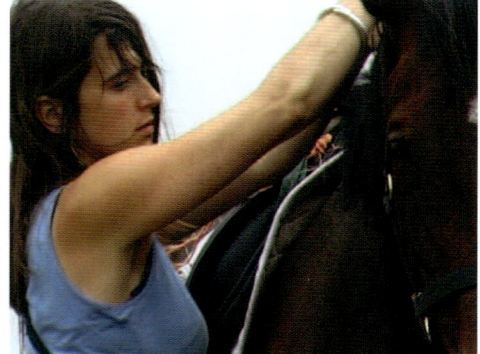
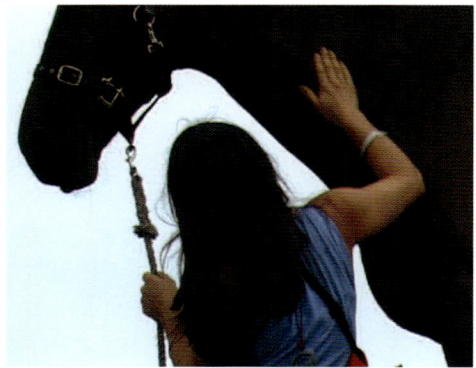

on horseback. What she was planning with Pippa, the other woman, was a ride from where Pippa lived in North Wales near Bala, back down to Barley's birth place and farm near here. So I was invited in that moment to make a film of them doing that. So I went off and learnt to ride, and then had to learn to ride one-handed with a camera! A year later we set off. We stayed with sheep farmers all the way down from North to Mid Wales over a period of about three weeks, which also was a great introduction for me to Wales, the Welsh language and the rural farming community here, which varies quite a lot even in that 170 mile relatively short distance.

Besides our own interaction with one another and the horses, which was quite complex (and I think something like three single mums with new babies, in terms of the level of discussion of health and hygiene and personality traits and dynamics amongst us and the animals), there was also the interaction with all our hosts, local farmers involved in a much more intense level dealing with animals, and whose riding skills alone put us to shame, because they were just so incredibly natural with their ponies. This particular moment in the film came about ten days into the ride. Barley's horse was only two, it was far too young to do the thing that we were doing really and was crazy all the time, and frightened of the bleat of a sheep, which in Wales is not ideal! But that particular moment, besides what it reflects I think about human interaction with a large beast, also really represented an unbelievable moment of extreme calm. The horse had not allowed us to leave it untethered at any point prior to that moment when it just stood in open moorland in that way. So the moment had an additional resonance for me within the struggle of the ride.

Sam: All of this is really fascinating, and reveals some of the many and varied ways in which non-human animals, and especially horses,

feature in human imaginations. Firstly, Anna mentioned not having had any contact with animals for a while, and therefore being drawn towards the prospect of re-engaging with animals and, by extension, nature. Horses are particularly useful mediators in this respect. They are domesticated and tame, but always retain an element of the wild – their fight or flight instinct is strong, and this seems to add to their allure in our 'industrialised' imaginations – at least those of us who are, through our lifestyle and livelihood, divorced from animals in their 'natural' state. They also enable us to transcend the boundaries of urban living and act as our guides as we re-enter the natural world. They literally carry us from one state to another.

Barley and Pippa had grown up with horses in rural areas where for many, and young people in particular, horses represent freedom – the ability to traverse otherwise inaccessible landscapes. Travelling on horseback is, as Anna notes, a unique way to see the countryside, but also to experience it. The phenomenological concept of 'being-in-the-world' takes on a new dimension if your 'being' is contingent on the sure-footedness and cooperation of another living creature. In the film, this mutual interdependence is clearly demonstrated. Barley's stroking of her horse is an attempt to calm him, but is also a means of communicating her dependence – he is an important member of the group, as without him, progress would be slow and much more arduous. For me, Barley's caresses communicate to the horse his importance, his crucial role in the realisation of this pilgrimage. Anna recognises this herself when she describes the ride as a struggle – it appears to be a rite of passage for both the women and their horses. Many anthropological commentators have observed that it is the journey which is the key element of a pilgrimage and it is whilst they are on the move that pilgrims find 'healing'. In this respect then, the horses enable healing – they facilitate and indeed make possible this reconnection with the land, mediating between the women and the environment. The horses are thus liminal beings, both wild and tame, cultured and natural.

However, horses are also potent symbols in many cultural contexts, and here is no exception. Anna referred to the Welsh farmers they encountered being 'natural' with their ponies. I have argued elsewhere that horses, and especially the indigenous Welsh ponies and cobs, are important markers of identity. As Heidegger would say, the farmers coexist with their horses in a great state of authenticity – in other words, their relationship with their horses is such that it is completely natural to them, an element of their being which they no longer have to think about – their interaction is almost instinctual, it just 'is' as a result of their shared existence. For the women in Anna's party, however, their inexperience or rustiness in the saddle made the act of being on the horse one of constant concern and interest. This is not to say that the farmers they encountered took their relationships with their horses for granted. On the contrary, their horses represented not just an extension of their habitus, but of their very selves.

Anna also referred to the women interacting with large animals (or 'beasts' to use Anna's phrase) who were, in size, temperament and 'nature', very different to themselves. Again, this is a theme which is well documented in the anthropological literature concerned with human interactions with other non-human animals – that animals represent a mirror, and in the reflection we see ourselves. How we (as individuals or as members of a particular 'culture') choose to interpret this reflection can be extremely informative. It is an accepted fact that in a 'Western' context, human interactions with other animals are predicated on control, but how we chose to exert that control again is particularly instructive. The farmers 'control' the horses they ride, but because it is a daily reality

for them, it doesn't necessarily arouse analysis or comment – they don't question the relationship, it just is. The women, however, were coming to terms with the need to exert some degree of control over their horses – Anna's use of the objectifying 'beast' exemplifies this, as does the occasion depicted in the film. It is the first time where the human rider is able to gain 'control' of the situation. However, what Barley's actions and Anna's narrative reveal is that these women find the idea of control difficult to come to terms with. Anna likens their interaction with the horses to the relationship between single mothers and their children. There is the recognition that while the maternal role is to ensure the behaviour of the child, i.e. it is controlling to some degree, the nature of the relationship is ultimately caring, seeking cooperation and mutual development rather than forced submission – it is based on trust as opposed to domination.

While Anna is setting up the next film, I just wanted to give a brief introduction to those of you who aren't familiar with social anthropology as an academic discipline, why it is that I'm particularly interested in human interactions with non-human animals, because the etymology of the word anthropology (anthropos and logos) demonstrates that anthropology is the study of humans. So why would I, as an anthropologist, be interested in non-human animals as well? It's only really in the last twenty years or so that the anthropological interest in the interactions that humans have with non-human animals has undergone close scrutiny, but that's not to say that anthropologists haven't been concerned with animals in the past, just that in traditional ethnographic research animals tended only to feature on the periphery as objects to human subjects. As a result, non-human animals constituted what Ardner has referred to as a 'muted group'. In other words, in a lot of ethnographic research, the presence of non-human animals was acknowledged but they weren't really considered as integral to the ethnographic process. However, and largely due to postmodern developments in the discipline, anthropological practitioners are coming to recognise that many humans exist in what you could refer to as inter-subjective, or at very least interactive, relationships with other animals, and that's certainly what Anna alluded to when she was talking about the relationship that she and her fellow riders had with the three horses. It wasn't just the three women on motorbikes, rather, the horses had personalities of their own [*turns to address Anna*] that were integral to your relationships with each other and the discussions that you had.

So consequently, we're starting to adopt a more reflexive approach which accepts that non-human animals play a much more active role in human social networks, and this has been largely influenced by the world views of traditional anthropological informants, cultures from around the world, who don't have an attitude towards animals that's based on a mechanistic Cartesian hierarchy (seeing other animals as machines) and Judeo-Christian teachings, and therefore animals are much more integrated within their social networks. In particular, many rituals revolve around animals, and transgressive animals in particular as we'll see in the next of Anna's films, *Begail Foxwell Whip*. Several of the animals featured here could be described as transgressive themselves, for example the crows who bite the tip off the lamb's tongue – they're transgressive because they encroach into human domestic realms and interfere with human activity. Many anthropologists who've done research into fox hunting, for example, argue that the fox is transgressive. It encroaches into the domestic sphere and takes livestock that are intended for human consumption, and that's why it has to be hunted in a particularly ritualised manner. So this leads me to my first question for Anna, and it's a question relating to social networks. I know from what I've seen of your previous work that it's been concerned with human social networks, so I wondered whether the project we're about to see, the *Begail Foxwell Whip*, is a continuation of that theme but with animals being acknowledged as social actors in these social networks, or at least within the social networks of the Welsh countryside.

Anna: I do think that animals are obviously essential to the people that I worked with and I was interested in finding out what levels of connection the teenagers had with animals. I wonder whether I might have romanticised that in my own mind before I started and thought that their interactions might be much more emotionally loaded or intimate than they actually were. There was a boy working with a flock of sheep, and a boy who works with sixty hounds. Each of these two could identify specific animals, which I could not identify at all, as individuals in a crowd, as their particular favourites, or ones that they had a particularly strong attachment to. But at the same time they knew that they were working animals and that they were going to get rid of them, or that they were passing through. So the animals in general are obviously what drives those people's everyday life and they spend a huge amount of time with them. In the case of the boy with the hounds, he surely spends more time with animals than he does with humans. With the title of the film *Begail Foxwell Whip*, I just took the job titles. Begail is the Welsh for shepherd. Foxwell in fact is just the surname of the falconer I worked with, but I loved the fact that a falconer was named Foxwell, and Whip is the name… I don't quite understand, you probably know what a whip refers to?

Sam: It's a member of the hunt staff who's responsible for keeping the hounds under control during hunting.

Anna: Right. So in the case of Begail and Whip, they're defined by their social interaction with animals. Shall we watch it then?

(*Begail Foxwell Whip* is shown to the audience)

Sam (addressing the audience): What I found particularly interesting in this film were themes of identity, of ritual, of place, but particularly themes of control. For all of Anna's informants, their engagements with animals were premised on control of those animals and I wondered whether their engagements with these animals were representative of their liminal status. They're liminal in the sense that they're adolescents, but they're also liminal in the sense that they're engaged with animals in activities that are regarded by wider society as transgressive, that they're not socially acceptable outside of the community in which they happen to reside at the moment. (Adressing Anna) So I wondered whether you thought that these were, that they were respective of their liminal status, but also whether their relationships with animals were illustrative of the liminality of rural communities in general.

Anna: Just give me that last bit again?

Sam: Well, whether the fact that they're all engaged in what are, effectively, hunting activities, and the way that they're engaging with these animals is representative of their liminal status themselves as adolescents, but also when we talked earlier you said that Holly, for example, had a life outside of this particular activity but she kept it very separate.

Anna: Yeah, that's true. Holly the falconer is a hairdresser, so most of her week is spent cutting and dyeing people's hair, and I did really

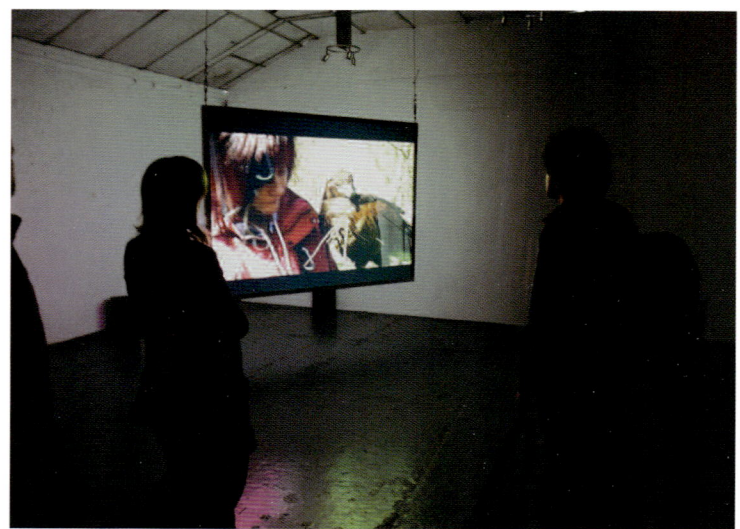

enjoy the images of her own hair, with the feathers of the falcon, there was just something really great about that. But yes, she reiterated to me that she essentially is a regular seventeen year old girl who's a hairdresser and goes out with her mates on a Saturday night. It just happens to be that on a Sunday, or in any of her other free time, she has this passion for working with the birds, and it's her aunt and uncle who run a falconry centre in the Black Mountains. It was clearly something that she had a lifelong commitment to. It was very difficult to find a teenager who does work with birds because what it transpires is if you own a bird you have to fly it three or four times a week and it will survive sixteen to twenty-five years and longer in the case of bigger birds, so for a teenager to make that kind of commitment is a pretty major thing. So she was quite unique, I think, in being as young as she is and having the level of experience that she does. So on one hand she could have been very proud of her expertise and very keen to share it with the rest of her hairdressing or friendship community, and she chose it seemed to keep it quite separate or private. I couldn't work out whether it was her judging them as being not interested, or her having tried to explain and her friends not understanding. I wasn't quite sure, but she was clearly very well respected and quite well known within the falconry community.

The boy working with the hounds had been really badly bullied at school in England, so he found the community here a very much easier and more welcoming one because I think it is a lot more acceptable to be a whip in a rural and more agricultural community. He'd grown up as a farmer, but really had been a one-off in his school environment, so he'd really had a history of struggling with this kind of passion. He was very private, and he was quite ashamed I felt, in that he didn't want me to watch him gutting the animals (they call them casualties) that the farmers bring to then feed to the dogs. And he kept asking me had I filmed everything I wanted to, and of course I hadn't, so I kept going, 'well, I'd be quite interested to just hang on for a little while…?' I realised after a while that that would have been a boundary too far, to ask to witness that, because he really was not wanting to share that. I wasn't really able to talk to him about what it represented for him. But he was clearly really proud of his position within the hunt, where he's dressed up in all the gear, cravat or something, and obviously galloping across the fields and gaining a huge amount of respect within that community for what he does. So I think it's something that has to be kept very private in certain contexts and it can be openly celebrated in others, and I think that even the very young are very well aware of that.

With Ioan, the lambing boy, he doesn't really talk about his interest at school but he really sweetly described a friend of his that he goes rabbitting with, as his partner. I really liked the way he described him as his partner, the collaborative nature of what they do when they're rabbitting. I guess that was really expressed in that term. I guess that was also indicative of young people finding individuals who trust and understand their level of engagement with animals, but it's not necessarily whole groups of people.

Sam: That brings me on to the level of engagement with animals that Holly in particular had, that she was very aware of the need to think like an animal, to get inside the animal's head, if the relationship was going to be productive and successful. And she also made an important comment that the relationship was contingent on respect, that she had to have respect for the hawk and its boundaries and needs, and in return it would respect her. And that reminded me of a point made by an anthropologist, Tim Ingold, who suggested that traditionally hunting is an intersubjective relationship that's contingent on trust and contingent on the hunter being able to empathise with, or think like, an animal. He's talking about the animistic beliefs of 'traditional' hunter-gatherers and reindeer herders and argues that once the focus shifts from hunting for subsistence to keeping domestic animals for food, or hunting for recreation, that relationship becomes based on dominance rather than trust, and I thought that Holly's case was a particularly interesting example of that – there's the respect there, but it's also a relationship based on domination, in that the hawk is kept tethered and is only allowed to fly and hunt in conjunction with its human carer or trainer. And so while there was an element of respect, the relationship was very hierarchical and I thought that leads into the next film that you're going to show, so did you want to introduce it?

Anna: Yes, I will. I was just going to say something about economics as well. With the control and dominance in those cases with the animals, particularly the falcons, they are radio tagged, because they're so valuable. Just the Harris hawk, which is quite a common and a lower level falcon, is worth something like two thousand pounds, so they have an economic need to make sure that the birds don't just head off. And there's a big business, particularly with Saudi Arabians trading falcons on a phenomenal financial level, and that was also reflected in the jesses – the world of falconry has also hugely informed language and there are lots of phrases that they explained to me are used in everyday language that come from falconry, and its really annoying that I can now not remember the name for all… the hoods… there was something to do with falling over drunk as well, but I can't remember which of the phrases refers to that! So, it was just that there was this economic tethering or need to keep them close in that case.

Sam: And I suppose the same could be said for the shepherd as well, that the dominant reason for the relationship with sheep is an economic one.

Anna: It theoretically would be, but in the case of that family, they chose to maintain the flock despite it not making any money, because they had access to a space and because Ioan had showed such aptitude at a young age, that they were really keen to encourage him. Last year they lost money because they picked the wrong time to take the lambs to the market. This year he said that he was going to get more pocket money, but I think it really is operating on a pocket money basis, more than anything else. So it really is a labour of love, rather than an economy. They've only got three hundred sheep. It sounds as though you really need to have numbers in the thousands and be out in the hills really in this area to make money from sheep. And the cost of all the wool from all the three hundred sheep was only enough to pay the guys that sheared them and pay for the blades

to be sharpened – there's no additional profit on the wool from three hundred sheep, so it's quite a tough economic balance.

While I've been working on *Begail Foxwell Whip*, which has been quite a short project, I've also been working on a much longer-term project with a company called Commissions East, who commission really interesting site-specific projects mainly in the East of England. I was invited to respond to the four hundred year commemorations of the British leaving the East of England to go to Virginia USA prior to the Founding Fathers, in 1606. As part of my research I met an anthropologist in Chelmsford who was really passionate about Pocahontas, the Indian Princess, and so I was sitting in on a rainy Thursday in Chelmsford with this old guy, with a Pocahontas doll figure behind him, and he told me everything about Pocahontas. And he knew the chiefs of the tribes in Virginia, and I found it so amazing that she had captured his imagination and that he wasn't a nine year old girl! Pocahontas provided a really good false protagonist for me, for exploring the state of Virginia, so I used her as my virtual guide and travelled 'with her' or looking for her for a month. I'm just going to show you a four and half minute split screen piece that goes alongside a much more comprehensive forty minute single screen piece that will describe the story of Pocahontas much more thoroughly, so this is quite an open response, loosely based on this kind of false search for Pocahontas. She was a young girl when the first settlers arrived in Virginia from Britain, and she was responsible, it seems, for bridging the cultural gap between the British and her own native people. She learnt English, converted to Christianity, married an English man and came over to Britain, so whatever you read into why she might have done that, and the documentary explains, or questions that, in a nutshell that is why we still know about her.

Sam: And for me as well I guess in relation to the previous film that was shown, there's some reoccurring themes again: the themes of identity, of ritual, of place and of control – control of the environment and within the environment.

Anna: The other thing I should say is that I was in Virginia in November, in autumn, so I've kind of got Halloween and Thanksgiving topping and tailing my visit, and it was the hunting season and that really hugely informed what I was filming. Besides looking for Pocahontas, I was looking for situations that occur now in America that might also have been occurring four hundred years ago, at the time when the settlers came.

(Anna shows *Little White Feather and the Hunter*)

Sam: For me personally, this film was illustrative of the dichotomy between the indigenous engagements with animals, at the end there you saw the tribute ceremony in honour of the deer, and the descendents of the colonists who are hunting in a more recreational sense. I found the hanging deer particularly emblematic of that conflicting relationship, and perhaps as a metaphor for the indigenous communities who were destroyed by the colonists if you

like. Was that something that occurred to you as you were making the film?

Anna: I tend to make work quite instinctively, so as I said, I was kind of following the lead of Pocahontas, and had seen that it was the hunting season and wanted to follow what I could relating to the hunting. But it was only when I got back that I thought along the lines of 'Oh, maybe there's a fable, or maybe Pocahontas is a deer, or not quite as explicitly as that, but is there a kind of tie-in there?' But I'm open to readings, and I recognise that seeing a deer hung up in that way in a tree is quite a powerful image for anybody. But I'm quite… I'd be reticent to put any particular label on it myself, partly because a month is an extraordinarily limited amount of time to understand Virginian, or American, history and culture, and particularly the extremely complex and sophisticated relationships between the native American tribes and the non-native American peoples *and* their relationships with animals, so it's quite involved to try unpicking. But one thing I would say is that it was quite easy to go in with a certain expectation, and that was quite quickly overturned. So, for example, the guy hanging the

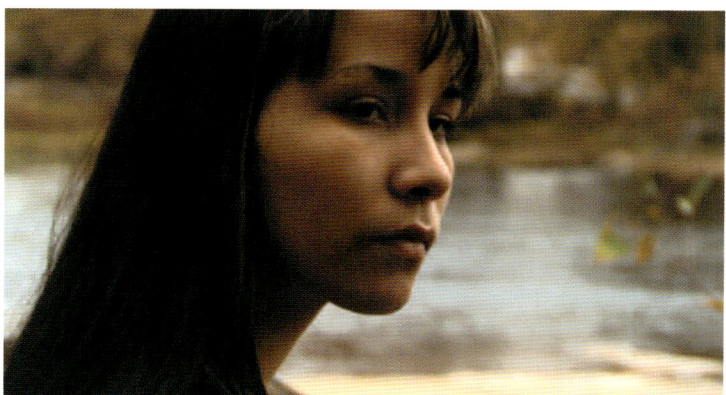

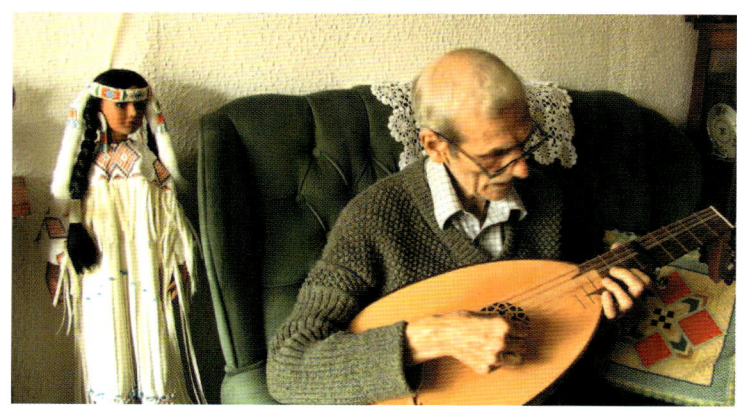

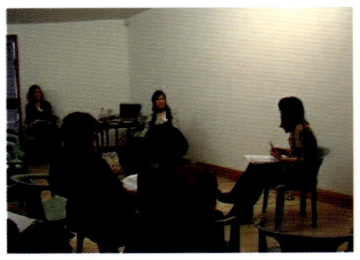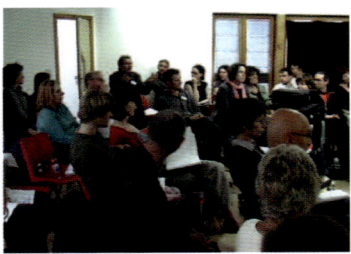

deer in the tree is not a recreational hunter – he's hunting because he's not a rich man and he's using that season to get as much meat in the freezer as he can. So he was out at dawn every day. The season's quite short, you can use a bow and arrow for a while, and then you can move on to guns, and you can only shoot certain deer at certain times. The whole season I think only lasts about five or six weeks, so it's quite a limited time. We went to the butcher with him, and it was clear that he was a really talented hunter – the butcher was like 'Whoa, that old guy really knows what he's doing.'

I noticed elsewhere when I was out looking for hunters elsewhere, it didn't feel like a recreational sport, it felt like quite poor people trying to get food, actually. I'm sure there's a recreational element as well, of course, but it seemed double-edged. And then with the tribute ceremony, that tribute is given as payment of tax. There are only two recognised tribes in Virginia, and those are the two that give a tribute, so there was a deer coming from each one, and they were giving the tribute to the governor, and in return they get their reservation. They're really complex issues, but I'm open to whatever readings people bring.

Sam: That's probably a good time to throw it open.

Audience member: I wonder whether one of the questions that's thrown up is the relationship between these activities and the contexts and situations of war, and the relationship between agriculture and war as well. I think some of those questions seemed to be raised for me particularly in relation to the hunt, which is a ritual strongly connected with the social hierarchies that then manifest in wartime: the officer class, the fighting men and the prize of running to ground one's enemy. It's obvious enough, but I think more fundamentally, the relationship, the idea of agriculture itself as having a warlike element to it, a war on the environment, whereby, for example, if we look at the indigenous people, tribal hunter gathering people, wherever they may be living, and agricultural societies. That element of continuity with the environment is sacrificed when society becomes an agricultural, rather than a hunter-gatherer, society and to that extent, war is an internal psychic event as well.

Sam: Yes, many anthropologists certainly recognise the link between 'hunting' and war, with the quarry being seen as an enemy to be eradicated, or at least outwitted. Commentators throughout history have noted that human beings seem to have an innate desire to hunt, and in some cases, such as in times of war, the quarry becomes other human beings. In terms of the shift from a hunter-gatherer lifestyle to an agricultural mode of subsistence, as I mentioned earlier, Ingold sees this as a shift from trust to domination in terms of the ways in which humans think about, and engage with, other animals. Modern forms of pastoralism such as ranching and industrialised agriculture result in objectification as well as domination, and we certainly see this during times of human conflict – the enemy is portrayed as inhuman, and this provides justification for many horrific acts of violence.

Hamish Fyfe: Just to ask Sam, you alluded to the personality of animals and I wonder how much in terms of, I suppose both of your works, was struggling against, and also attempting to construct an anthropomorphic understanding here. Do you use the term personality with all its cultural connotations for us knowingly in relation to the existence of animals?

Sam: I think personhood is probably a better term to use than personality and anthropomorphism is a complex issue that has been quite widely debated in anthropology. An anthropologist called Kay Milton has come up with an alternative term – 'egomorphism' – because she argues that anthropomorphism maintains a hierarchy between human and non-human animals by attributing characteristics that a person thinks are exclusively human to animals, whereas egomorphism is the recognition that things other than humans can have a personhood, that they're actually like us as individuals rather than appearing to be human-like, so perhaps personhood is a better term to use than personality.

Audience member: This is just an observation really. I'm really interested in the children that keep these relationships with animals quite private, quite secret, and I wonder whether it's because most children's relationships with animals are kind of mediated through film, television and Hollywood versions of relations with animals and that a lot of these young people that we've seen in your film actually have very mature relationships with those animals. They're actually doing a job of work, you know, helping a sheep have a lamb, and then swinging it round to get the air in, and castrating… and I've done all that and its very real, you know, the life and death of a lamb in front of you is very, very real and you have a particular relationship with that sheep if you rear them. And I just wonder if it's because it just sets them apart somehow from most children's experience of *101 Dalmations*, or soft and cuddly, fluffy

relationships with animals, which actually aren't genuine. There's some kind of integrity about seeing that boy work with those animals and I just think it's very interesting that privacy, that secrecy, that I think is actually not very child-like, it's actually a mature response and a respectful relationship with animals.

Audience member: It also reflects our times, because thirty, forty, fifty

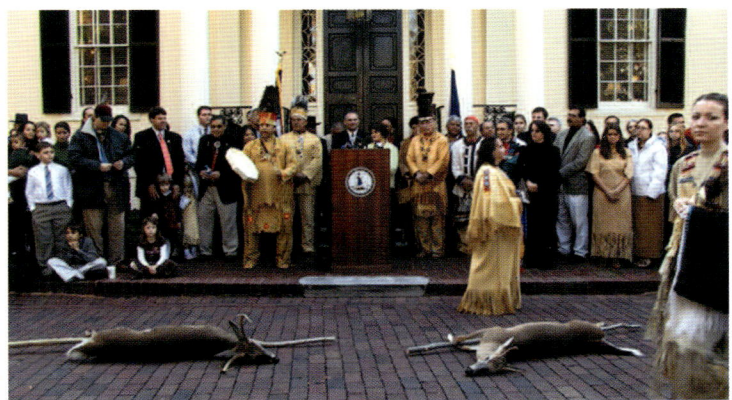

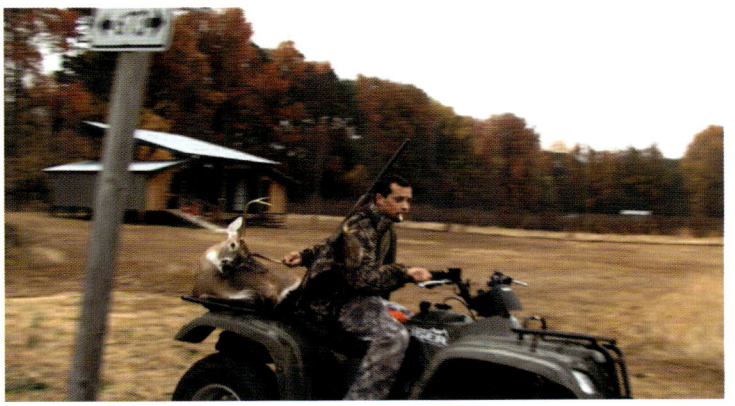

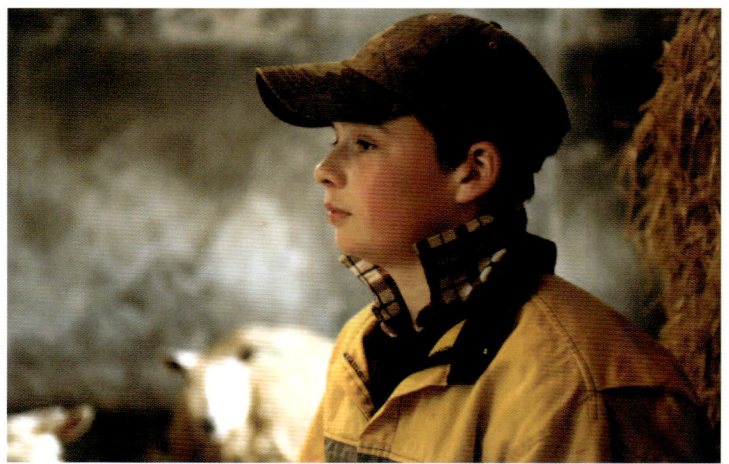

kids that are actually doing the work with the animals, they're not part of Young Farmers! So even Young Farmers is a completely different kind of organisation about something else, and again Sam you might know how that's different?

Sam: It's a social networking kind of thing, a club where children from farming families and rural areas in general go to socialise. In Wales in particular, the Welsh language plays an important part, and so kids whose parents farm go to the Young Farmers to socialise but also to learn skills or to improve on skills that they may already have. There is some element of animal husbandry involved, as there will be workshops held where the YFC members have to judge animals at a mock agricultural show, but for the young people who are already involved with the animals in their day-to-day lives, there are other arenas and opportunities for them to develop or show off their skills, such as through the breed societies, or the hunts.

Anna: I didn't really understand it, but it didn't seem as though Ioan had anything to do with Young Farmers, quite clearly! I don't know how else you would describe him…

Heike: How did they respond to seeing themselves portrayed in this way, did they engage with the film that you made?

Anna: Just Ioan's family came yesterday, the sheep farmer family. Holly lives in the Black Mountains, which is quite far away, and I had a sense with James, the other boy, that he wasn't going to come. He's seventeen and he's working full time down the road and it would be quite a brave thing, I think, to just show up. So I haven't heard their responses, I've yet to send them the film. Bobby talked a lot to Ioan and his family last night and gave me some really

years ago those children wouldn't have been abnormal in our society in any way shape or form and the fact that our society is becoming less accepting of rural life, and that film to me made me feel quite confused in some way because I live in a rural area where that sort of thing still happens all the time, and my sister's a farmer and both their children work on the farm. They're teenagers and they form their own communities within the farming community and I think they still feel rather separate from the rest of society and I think more and more so as life becomes less accepting of that. And seeing that offered as a piece of art, where in fact it's a reality for a lot of people, although less a reality now, is a way of bridging those societies.

Anna: It was really interesting to me calling the Young Farmers which was my first port of call, thinking that will obviously be where to find the teenagers working with working animals, and I was told that the Young Farmers didn't really have any farmers that were working with working animals and so it seemed as though the interesting feedback about his confidence and how he felt pride in seeing himself doing his work.

Sam: This discussion could have taken so many turns, and covered a multitude of themes, but the points which were raised are, I think, at the heart of human relations with other animals, and, ultimately, what it means to be human. We engage with other animals in almost every aspect of our day-to-day lives – the food we eat, the clothes we wear, the medicines and toiletries we use are all dependent on our relationships with other animals. Yet in contemporary UK society the vast majority of the population keeps these practical relationships at arm's length – we distance ourselves from animals and practices deemed 'animalistic' such as hunting. Indeed, most of us understand other animals through pets or media representations and second hand information. As has been noted above, the young people in Anna's projects are both exceptions and exceptional. They belong to a minority of people who know what it is like to work with animals and to rely on that relationship in a very real sense. Yet their skills are not deemed valuable or necessarily desirable by their peers nor indeed the society at large. Rural traditions are, in many cases, dying out because they are not taken up and embraced by young people in rural communities, yet, as the case of *Paloma Ceffyl* demonstrated, these traditions and the ritual elements accompanying them (such as riding a horse to travel across the country) serve to reunite us with our past, and with nature, and ultimately with ourselves.

Anna Lucas

Begail Foxwell Whip

Video Installation
16mm film transferred to DVD
colour stereo 7 mins 30 seconds

Pendre Art Gallery, Cardigan
Friday 23rd – Saturday 31st May 2008

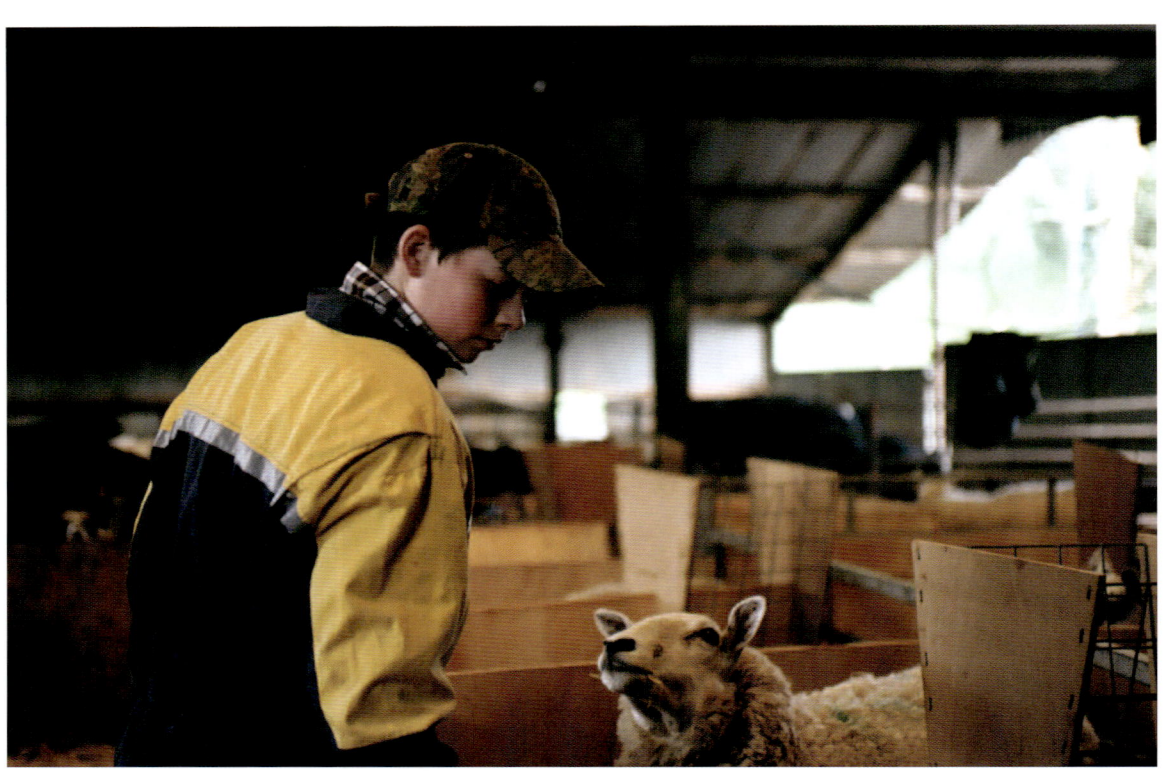

BEGAIL OEN

The worst thing we've had is crows
yeah
taking the…
when we were lambing out.
Because of the room we were lambing out
about two years ago,
no, more than that
and erm… the lamb's head was out.
The crows were coming.

The ewes were stretched out pushing
but the crows were taking the tip of the tongue.
And then when the lambs were getting stronger they couldn't suck
because they didn't have the front of the tongue to pull the teat.
So we were losing all of them then.
They were getting hungry and nothing happened.
And they were dying or we would have to adopt.

So a chap and dad went down then and he told dad
'meet me here eight o'clock tonight'.

And the two of them were on the field at eight
and the two big ravens were there too.
And they went down and the ravens flew.
And they stayed there until eleven o'clock
until the ravens came back again and
the two of them had 'em.
Big ravens.
And then it never happened again then.

Ioan Jones
Berllan Dywyll, March 2008

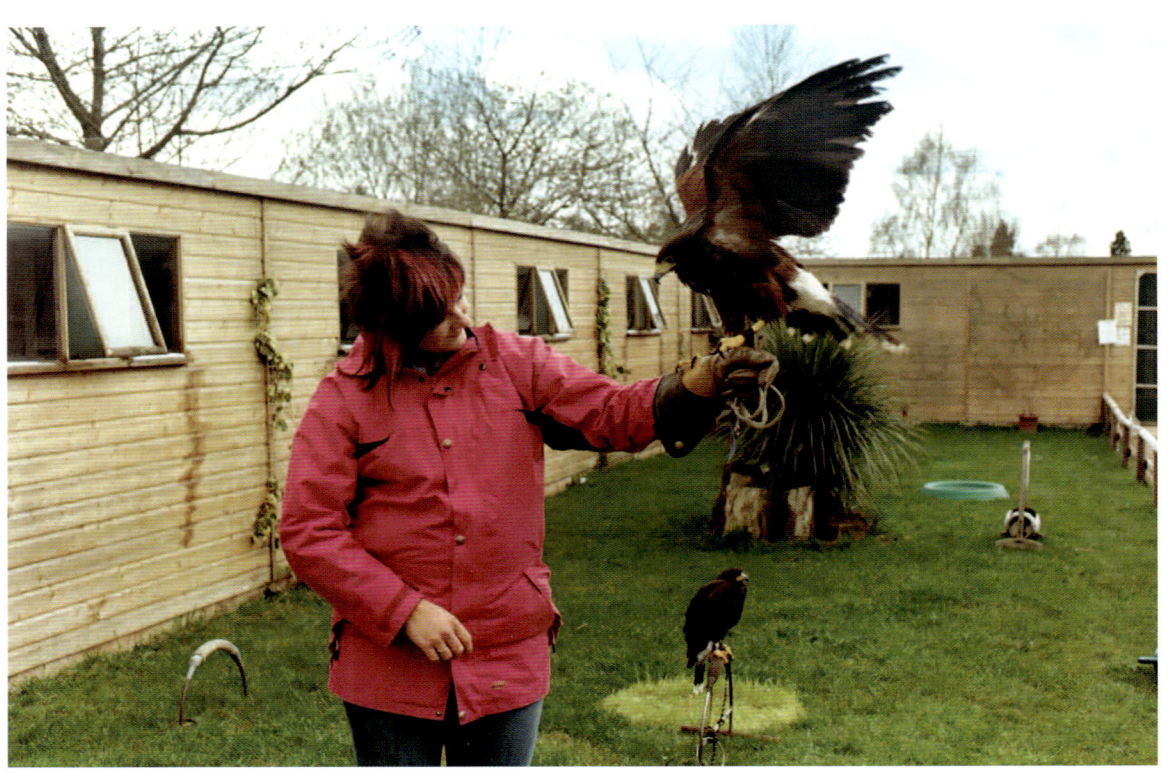

FOXWELL

In the wild they are usually from the desert areas, like Mexico, things
like that.
And, well they are the second most successful pack hunter in the world
this Harris Hawk.
You get the females that sit up on top of the cactus just waiting and you
get the little males that run around on the cactus floor pushing out the
hares, and the rabbits.
And as soon as the hare or the rabbit breaks cover the big females will
peel over then
and go in and they'll all share dinner together.

The noises they was just makin', they talk to each other like that.
And its almost like they got their own language, they talk to each other
and then they'll move around together and work together.
The little males will be sort of down in the bottoms of the trees, and
the females will be on top.
As soon as the rabbit breaks cover, goes out into an open field, the big
females'll peel over then.
The dogs sort of sniff around in the bushes and the dogs will go on
what you call point.
English setters are famous for it. Which they stay absolutely still.
We had a dog on for twenty minutes and they don't move a muscle.

You wait 'til the bird gets in the right position and then you wait on and
wait on
until you tell the dog to go in and flush the rabbit.
It goes in then and the birds come down.
So it waits and waits and waits until you tell it to push it out.
They do work well together.

Holly Foxwell
Black Mountain Falconry, March 2008

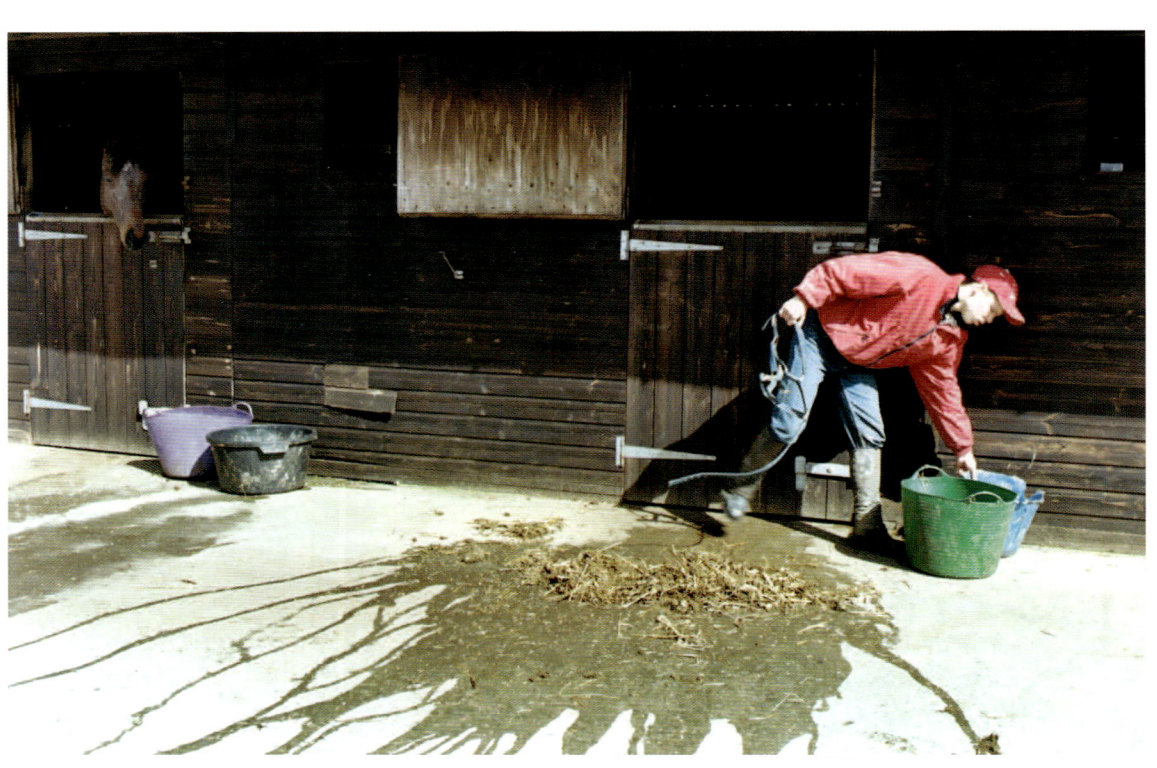

WHIP

That calf's completely dead now
It's just the nerves and things making it kick.

James Jeavons
Cefn Lodge, March 2008

Iain Biggs

The Presence of Absence: Song, Ritual, and Place

This essay is in two parts – the first is an argument about the relevance of old and often overlooked or ridiculed elements of popular culture; the second a loosely woven presentation of song lyric fragments and images that parallels concerns expressed in the first.

Drawing on a range of sources including cultural geography, critical regionalism in its broader sense and place-oriented visual arts, the essay makes two main points. Firstly, certain types of old, quasi-pagan songs still live on in pockets of contemporary vernacular consciousness, and in doing so offer us the opportunity to remember a quasi-pagan sense of place and community. As such they serve as 'spectral traces' that haunt the present; revenants brought alive by singers that can be experienced through testimonial imagination as witnessing a past that might still impact on the present. In this way they can contribute to an urgent and fundamental cultural reorientation that will become necessary if we are to face the psycho-social challenges of major environmental change. The second point is that we need to pay greater attention to singing or hearing certain songs – that is, to singing and listening as an articulation of testimonial imagination that almost becomes an everyday type of ritual, one that might help us better to understand our communal place. Believing that we need to live between enchantment and critical understanding, the text and images suggest that these songs model another sense of community in their ability to simultaneously enchant and remember absence and finitude.

Presenoldeb Absenoldeb: Cân, Defod a Lle

Mae'r erthygl hon mewn dwy ran – yn y rhan gyntaf ceir dadl am berthnasedd hen elfennau o ddiwylliant poblogaidd sydd yn aml yn cael eu diystyru neu eu gwawdio; yn yr ail ran ceir plethwaith llac o eiriau caneuon a delweddau sy'n adleisio'r hyn a geir yn y rhan gyntaf.

Gan dynnu ar ystod o ffynonellau, gan gynnwys daearyddiaeth ddiwylliannol, rhanbarthiaeth feirniadol yn ei hystyr ehangach, a'r celfyddydau gweledol sy'n ymwneud â lleoliad penodol, mae'r erthygl yn gwneud dau brif bwynt. Yn gyntaf, bod mathau penodol o hen ganeuon lled-baganaidd yn fyw o hyd ar lafar gwlad, ac felly yn ein hymwybyddiaeth, a'u bod yn rhoi cyfle i ni gofio'r ymdeimlad lled-baganaidd o le a chymuned. Maent felly'n 'olion rhithiol' sydd ar gerdded yn y presennol, yn cael eu hatgyfodi gan gantorion. Gallwn eu profi drwy ddychymyg sy'n tystio i orffennol a allai gael effaith ar y presennol. Trwy hyn gallant gyfrannu at newid gogwydd diwylliannol yn sylfaenol, a hynny ar frys, a fydd yn angenrheidiol os ydym am wynebu her seico-gymdeithasol newid amgylcheddol mawr. Yr ail bwynt yw bod angen inni roi rhagor o sylw i ganu neu glywed rhai mathau o ganeuon penodol – hynny yw, canu a gwrando fel ffordd o fynegi'r dychymyg tystiolaethol sydd bron yn mynd yn ddefod gyffredin – un a allai ein helpu i ddeall yn well ein lle yn y gymuned. Yn seiliedig ar y gred fod angen inni fyw rhwng swyngyfaredd a dealltwriaeth feirniadol, mae'r testun a'r delweddau yn awgrymu bod y caneuon hyn yn cyfleu ymdeimlad arall o gymuned oherwydd eu bod yn gallu ein swyno, ac ar yr un pryd ddwyn i gof absenoldeb a meidroldeb.

When Ruth Jones invited me to speak about ritual and community in public art at the *Holy Hiatus* symposium I turned to the quasi-pagan world of the old Borders ballads to address the symposium's concerns. I did so partly as one turns to old and reliable friends and in part because there is an uncanny correspondence between the world of those old songs and contemporary concerns with community. The cultural geographer John Wylie writes:

> We do not simply disappear when we turn into ghosts, Jacques Derrida (1994) notes; rather we pass into and are incorporated by other states and forms. Against any phenomenological naturalism that would confine human perception and presence to living, breathing, organic flesh, Derrida argues that 'the body' and its sensibilities are always a matter of prosthetics, augmentations, displacements, substitutions – different 'appearances of flesh'.[1]

The ballads that interest me confuse and destabilize the orthodox categories of identity by constructing a narrative world that challenges and subverts fixed distinctions between the human and non-human; between humans and animals or the 'good neighbours' (the fairies); and between the living and revenants (the dead returned not as ghosts but as physically embodied beings). A world, that is, in which the human body and its sensibilities are always potentially subject to liminal augmentation, to displacement and substitution, to different appearances of flesh. In such a world there must be many 'different appearances' of community and, in consequence, these songs suggest that in difficult times we may be sustained, as their first singers were, by a sense of a communality that, while displaced, substituted, or absent, is in consequence no less real.

My concern with 'supernatural' Borders ballads is, then, with their ability to bring into the living, breathing present of contemporary singing and listening direct traces of the values of these other kinds of communality; with their enacting a sonic *communal place to be* that is a spur to testimonial imagination.[2] I believe that, as such, they can help us reconfigure our understanding of community. This belief is based on the now familiar ritual of listening to these songs, turning them over on the tongue and in mindfulness, of finding their rhythms in the rhythm of my own walking. Or, to put this another way, of coming to live empathetically with the interwoven, multiple and absent communities present in those ballads and their associated landscapes.

We have a fundamental need for community. Yet it seems to me we also have surprisingly little sense of how this is to be met at a time when the traditional process of self-identification with a place-based community – urban or rural – becomes increasingly problematic. How are we to be 'at home' in a hybrid world of mass communication, virtual spaces and a proliferation of 'non-places'?[3] For many of us that traditional sense of place-based community is present in our lives only on account of its loss. However, this need not be seen as either a cause for regret and nostalgia, or as a justification for frenetic consumption of new technologies supposed to 'bring us together'. Instead it may be taken as a spur to reorient the dominant mentality, one pathologically subservient to the politics of consumerism, through practices of testimonial imagination that allow us to experience community differently, to be more self-sufficient because less literal in our understanding. This reorientation will, I believe, become absolutely necessary if we are to face the psycho-social challenges of major environmental change. Before we can address such fundamental questions, however, we must each discover how to live responsibly between those multiple communities, both present and absent, to which we are currently related in one way or another.

We have for some time lived in a world where it is taken for granted that successful professionals – artists and academics as much as business people – must move across the globe and between a plurality of cultures and locations. Ironically, this assumption about professional success depends on a highly *localized* sense of 'at-home-ness' derived from conformity to specific cultural and professional practices, norms, discourse, values and choices. 'At-home-ness' in this case depends on subscribing to the values of those globally dispersed institutional networks that authorise professional identity and facilitate success. In terms of the art world, for example, the resulting situation is typified by Miwon Kwon's observation that 'the success and viability' of professional work is measured in terms of 'the accumulation of frequent flyer miles'.[4]

Miwon Kwon's reputation as a curator and theorist is linked to her critique of 'place-bound identities'. It is a critique that requires a certain – and necessary – critical detachment from, and disenchantment with, the values of the majority of ordinary Americans. I have no quarrel with this necessary detachment of critical thinking. However, seen from an everyday perspective such detachment often masks a lack of concern for the specifics of environmental problems. This is the case with Kwon in so far as she fails to acknowledge, as arguably a reflexive practitioner of critical thinking should, the social and environmental impact of her professional viability and success as a 'radical' professional. Her 'blindness' in this respect is typical of the self-interest masked as critical detachment or 'disenchantment' upon which so much contemporary professional practice is in fact predicated. As such it is wholly consistent with Kwon's reading of Kenneth Frampton's ecologically oriented critical regionalism as 'dated', as 'out of sync with the prevalent description of contemporary life as a network of unanchored flows'.[5] Consistent because her reading appears to be self-interestedly 'blind' to the fact that the 'prevalent description' is itself a professionally adaptive projection of specific preoccupations; preoccupations that reflect the parochialism of a cosmopolitan professionalism. In this context Lucy Lippard suggests that those who identify themselves with the great cosmopolitan centers 'are among the most provincial people in the world'.[6] Today, however, such 'provincialism' has a direct and increasingly toxic effect on the global environment, one that may yet prove terminal to our species.

Kenneth Frampton's Critical Regionalism offers an alternative to this provincialism by orienting itself to the extra-professional issues of 'the primacy of grounded *ethical* practices which are ultimately concerned with "the way in which species-being conceives of its relation to nature, including its own nature".'[7] I have linked this approach to ethnographic research into vernacular music because we use songs – which have perhaps the most immediate affective force of all cultural artefacts – as a means to create (or recreate) 'homely' imaginal landscapes with temporal depth. Additionally, 'such landscapes can travel with people so as to give them a sense of "home" when they are not "at home"', just as a traveller may 'carry "home" around as a tangible point in fluidity'.[8] Re-experiencing old songs might, then, help us rethink a sense of community at home with the tensions within a Critical Regionalism that combines *both* an 'enchantment' derived from 'being-at-home' in the local *and* the 'disenchantment' necessary to critical thought.

Part One

My concerns here are by no means unique. They parallel those of artists like Christine Baeumler, Jane Bailey, Marlene Creates, Laura Denning, Ruth Jones, Daro Montag, Rowan O'Neil, Simon Read and Simon Whitehead; artists of various persuasions who have been quietly reconfiguring their practices in relation to questions thrown up by reconsiderations of culture, community and place. They practice an expanded Critical Regionalism that consciously embraces the ambiguities of living between multiple communities, making an *ethical commitment* to the necessary limits that stem from a concerned engagement with a particular locality or region and its communities. A commitment that entails freely accepting physical, professional and economical limitations that most contemporary artists reject as potentially inhibiting to professional success. At the root of this commitment is an acknowledgement of the ambiguous experience of presence and absence in relation to our multiple experiences of community. I understand these artists as deliberately refusing to make categorical 'either/or' choices between the very different, often apparently contradictory, values, memories, goals and understandings that underpin the different types of community and location to which we must all now relate. As I have argued elsewhere,[9] they may be said to have adopted an attitude of psychological (rather than theological) 'polytheism', one that links them to the concerns of the *Holy Hiatus* project and to the values embedded in old quasi-pagan Borders ballads. This polytheistic orientation is a positive response to the need to radically re-envisage how we are to be 'at-home' in a world of multiple and competing communities faced with the social upheaval that will inevitably follow major environmental change. The reason for this

may be suggested by something Henry David Thoreau wrote In his *Journal* of 1856: 'It would imply the regeneration of mankind if they were to become elevated enough to truly worship stocks and stones.'

If he who makes two blades of grass grow where one grew before is a benefactor, he who discovers two gods where there was only known the one before is a still greater benefactor. I would fain improve every opportunity to wonder and worship.

This polytheistic response also relates to questions of place/home. This is best illustrated by turning to Edward S. Casey's distinction between 'position' and 'place'; to his claim that 'If a position is a fixed posit of an established culture, a place, despite its frequently settled appearance is an essay in experimental living within a changing culture.'[10] Today any such genuine 'experimental essaying' of place requires us to engage ethically with a whole range of active agents – including perhaps non-human beings such as animals and trees – and not simply with our fellow human beings in a community given by a traditional sense of place. We need a polytheistic reconfiguring of our sense of 'at-home-ness' because we are always provisionally and experimentally placed between this multiplicity of agents and authoritative points of reference, both present and absent, from which we finally derive a sense of community.

Another way of looking at this same issue is by asking how then we are to understand the relationship between an immediate sense of place/community grounded in presence with all its enchantments (however temporary) on one hand; and the demands of critical reflection predicated on an understanding of absence and distance on the other. I share Jane Bennett's view that:

> Without modes of enchantment, we might not have the energy and inspiration to enact ecological projects, or to contest ugly and unjust modes of commercialization, or to respond generously to humans and nonhumans that challenge our settled identities.[11]

However, I would also argue that enchantment only informs an ethical sense of community if recognized as one pole in an endless oscillation between amazement and criticality, between a radical openness to the appearance of phenomena and an equally radical commitment to ethical concern grounded in the inevitability of absence. Certain Borders ballads have an uncanny capacity to perform just this oscillation as they are sung or heard, to enchant us while simultaneously reminding us of absence, of the loss of community. I would argue that these ballads serve a similar function to the memorial benches John Wylie discovers at Mullion Cove. They serve as audible reminders of the 'complex fashion' in which landscape, that coexistence of the 'visible and invisible, presence and absence, blindness and sight, love and loss', [12] is interwoven.

Old Songs and Another Thinking

My particular point of entry into rethinking the relation between art and community has been through Border ballads able to reactivate, for the duration of a song, the last active traces of an old polytheistic animism within British popular music culture.[13] These songs can be related to an expanded critical regionalism – a regionalism that adopts a vigorous critical solicitude to both global and local concerns and perspectives – because the polytheistic animism that permeates them 'is arguably not merely a religious preference but a distinct mode of thought and of universal organization' that promotes the ability to manage uncertainty. This ability is 'directly related' to polytheism's 'ultimate division of power and its lack of a single, omniscient figure of authority',[14] and so to the acceptance of ambiguity necessary to a form of living that experimentally essays all values in a changing culture.

The sung evocation of another, quasi-pagan, animistic way of thinking takes on a particular importance in the context indicated above. It offers an embodied potential point of resistance – activated through the shared community of singing and listening – to a social and cultural reductivism inseparable from the 'monotheistic individualism' presupposed by the forces that drive consumer society. Seen in the context of Marina Warner's writing on the culture of folk tales – where she claims that the primacy of metamorphosis in polytheistic animism 'runs counter to the notions of unique, individual integrity of identity in the Judaeo-Christian tradition'[15] – such songs remind us that there is nothing 'inevitable' about that presupposition or the secular commodity-based community into which that tradition has for the most part mutated. Historically these old ballads have already served as a focus of resistance in the early modern period in relation to the advent of the Protestant revolution's rationalization of theology in England and Scotland. They acted as a focus for popular resistance to a mentality that re-categorized men and women as 'witches' if they persisted in retaining the quasi-pagan, polytheistic, animistic world-view that these ballads perform, albeit often in a tacit form.

The 'supernatural' ballads are particularly relevant today partly because of their relation to the philosophical 'neo-animism' derived from Deleuze and Guattari and Actor Network Theory (ANT).

However, Hayden Lorimer, who draws selectively on these approaches, suggests another aspect of their value when he recognises that this neo-animism needs grounding in the language of vernacular observation that he associates with a range of subjugated, marginalised or forgotten cultural traditions and practices. Hence my engagement with Borders ballads seeks, among other things, to link the insights of academic theory with a practice that has a wider currency in larger communities. My use of the ballads coincides with Hayden Lorimer's concerns in this respect. It also coincides with Jane Bennett's concern with a 'quasi-pagan model of enchantment'[16] as a necessary corrective to the disenchantment from which large sections of the academic and art communities derive legitimacy and authority. Additionally, it links with John Wylie's argument that what he refers to as 'geographies of love' (those in which any real sense of community must be grounded) are predicated on 'a simultaneous *opening-onto* and *distancing from*'.[17]

It is important to note that the values played out in the Borders ballads are not isolated historical phenomena restricted to an archaic, local music. They are evoked in contemporary songs by singer/musicians as different as Alistair Roberts and Laura Veirs. This continuing song tradition challenges Yi-Fu Tuan's claim that issues of 'world and self', the 'fuzzy area where geography overlaps with religion', are necessarily framed by 'the spiritual longing to be elsewhere'; where '*elsewhere*' constitutes the 'unattainably far' community of an otherworldly heaven.[18] The significance of this challenge is best indicated via Rebecca Solnit's stress on the degree to which many Americans still imagine 'home' and 'homeland' in terms of the Judeo-Christian Eden, an identification typified by Thoreau's linking of the American backwoodsman with the biblical Adam.[19] If American presuppositions about 'home' and 'moving on' remain inseparable from the *mythos* of Genesis and the Fall, the American Dream and its place in global politics will continue to remain shadowed by a dualism predicated on notions of sin and expulsion from Paradise.

While Yi-Fu Tuan is correct in claiming that songs are virtual places, his emphasis on place in terms of pausing, resting, being nurtured is as questionable as his assumption that religion is synonymous with the root presuppositions and temporo-spatial assumptions of the monotheism of the Religions of the Book. In this context the supernatural Borders ballads act as *alternative places* when experienced as fluid, ongoing conversations between singers, as 'mutable text' and the telling of circumstances focused around a particular cluster of recurrent human concerns. They are valuable alternatives because, as Jane Bennett's identification of a particular relationship between song, enchantment and our relationship to 'home' suggests, they model a *conversational place* for the 'self' that is closer to Casey's definition of place referred to above than that of Yi-Fu Tuan. A sense of place in which the past is not only a shelter proffering a nostalgic sense of pause, rest, and nurture, but also a radical point of departure for experimental living within a changing culture.

Part Two

Each year I return to the southernmost edge of what is, historically speaking, the Borders region. This region produced, out of an isolated, violent and to us unimaginably insecure way of life, some of the Isle's most enduring vernacular songs. Rookhope, the focus of an old ballad called the 'Rookhope Ryde', is just over the hill from where my family stays each year. I began walking there because I married the granddaughter of a local woman. Weardale is not 'my' place and I do not 'belong' to the local community. However, over time, a whole vanished sense of community as evoked in song has entered my mind, heart and the rhythm of my walking. A particular sense of community that, although it finally faded as a lived experience from this hill country over the four hundred years ago, is remembered in old songs that have, at least for the most part, continued to mutate without losing all trace of the values that underpin their vision of the world.[20]

I offer below selected fragments of four old song lyrics and four images made while walking in the Borders region. Neither the fragments nor the images are selected on the basis of any literal equivalence or correlation to each other. Rather they are intended, in their juxtaposition, to invite you to listen to a present absence in line with the concerns indicated above. The images were made either in or around Weardale or else in the woodland that has grown along Scots' Dyke, the Elizabethan border ditch built in an attempt to finalise the border through the Debatable Land (where, in the summer of 2007, I made the observations that were eventually written up as follows):

In 1607 King James of Scotland, while campaigning in the Borders to end its violent culture of raiding and blackmail, hired a girl from Carlisle to sing him the old Borders songs. Some would have told of magic, revenants, and the 'good neighbours' – matters not fit for the ears of a good Christian King. She was paid twenty-eight shillings none the less. The past is not so easily made to conform to its usual telling here. Even into the twentieth century a few Cumbrian hill farmers still counted their sheep in Welsh, the last remembrance for a Wales that once dominated the west of the Isles. Some old songs have a mind of their own. At Scot's Dyke I cross and re-cross the blurred border now shrouded in a thin line of trees. It is still patrolled day and night – by rooks, hares, roe deer, owls and a pair of buzzards.

FOUR SONG FRAGMENTS

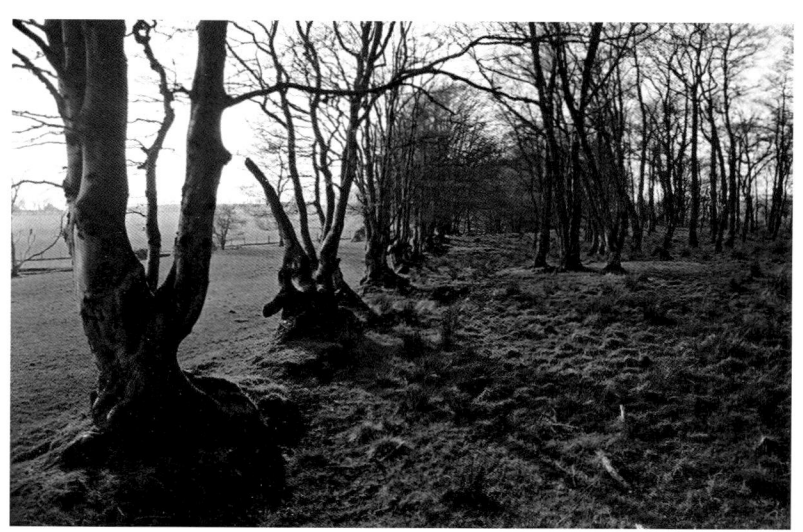

From 'In Our Lady's Name'

Oh I shall go into a hare
With sorrow and sighing and mickle care
And I shall go in his good name
Yes, till I be fetched home.
Hare, take heed for a bitch greyhound
Will harry thee all these fells around
For here come I in Our Lady's name
All but for to fetch you home.

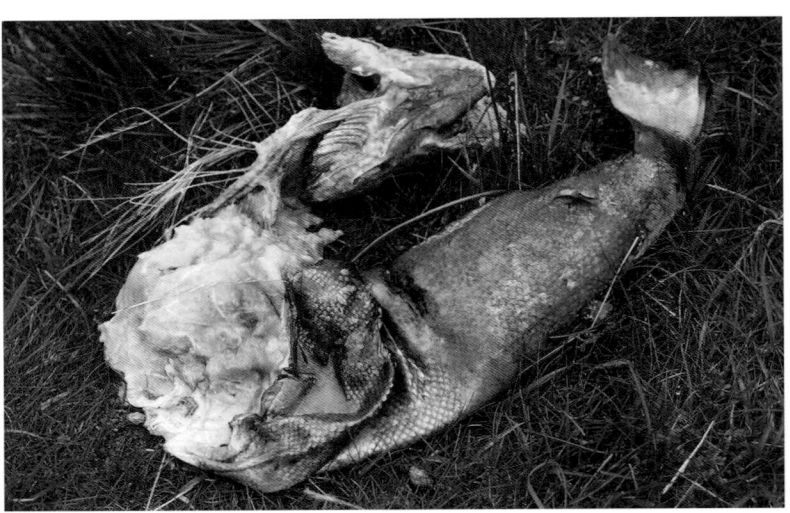

From 'Cruel Mother'

Oh bonny babe pray tell to me
The sun shines down on Carlisle Wall
The sort of death I shall have to die
And the lion shall be lord of all.

Seven years a fish, fish in the flood
The sun shines down on Carlisle Wall
Seven years a bird, bird in the wood
And the lion shall be lord of all.

Seven years a tongue to the warning bell
The sun shines down on Carlisle Wall
Seven long years in the flames of hell
And the lion shall be lord of all.

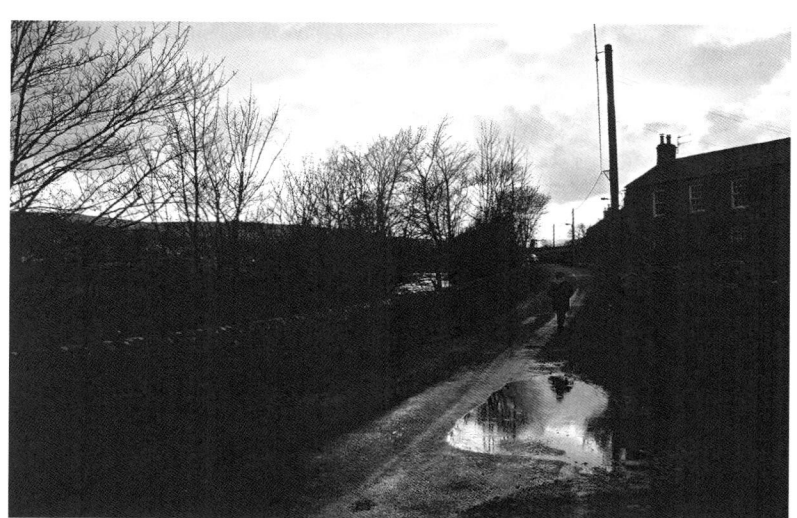

From 'Tam Lin'

'This night is Halloween, Janet,
The morn is Hallowday,
And if you'd dare your true love win,
You have no time to stay.'

'O tell me, tell me good Tam Lin
O tell me and tell me true;
Tell me this eve, an make no lie,
 What way I'll borrow you?'

'The night it is good Halloween
When Elfish folk will ride,
And they that wad their true-love win
At Miles Cross they must bide.'

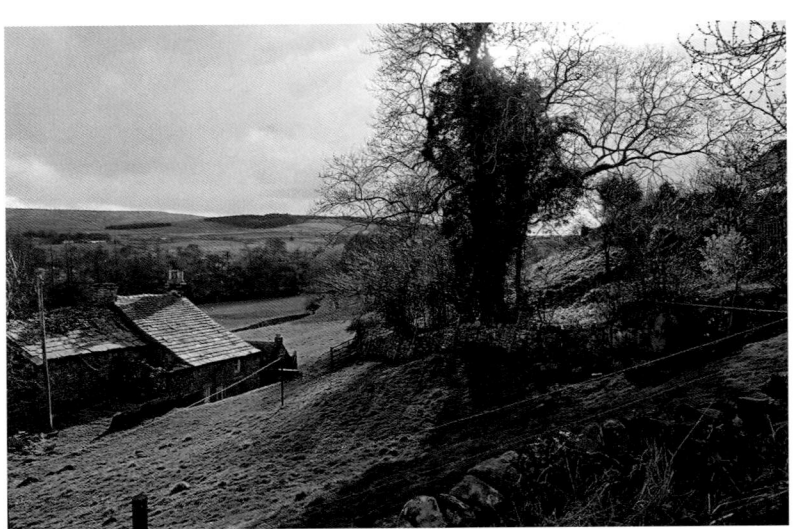

From 'Twa Sisters'

Then out of the woods came a fiddler fair
Oh the wind and rain
He plucked thirty strands of her long yellow hair
Crying 'oh the dreadful wind and rain'
And he made a fiddle bow of her long yellow hair
Oh the wind and rain
Made a fiddle bow from her long yellow hair
Crying 'oh the dreadful wind and rain'.

Last Thoughts

Janet Wolff raises the problem of taking the material of the Borders ballads literally in connection with Tony Harrison's poetry-performance work *Bow Down*, which takes the 'Twa Sisters' as its starting point. She objects to the 'horrendous fantasies of male violence', including the torture and death of the older sister, that Harrison derives from the ballad.[21] Some versions of the 'Twa Sisters' 'are violently, even sadistically, misogynistic. However, I would suggest that it is a mistake to take these songs at face value since all exist in many versions, a good number of which actually subvert or counter the authority of a misogynistic orthodoxy, while simultaneously acknowledging its social force.

In most versions of the 'Twa Sisters' sung today (many of which are very old) the focus is on the ritual dismemberment of the body of the younger sister to provide materials for the construction of a stringed instrument, either a harp or fiddle. To me this surreal passage is the crux of the song, located both within and somehow to one side of the main narrative. Rather than a literal (and so absurd) account of dismemberment, I hear it as evoking the murdered girl's metamorphosis from one kind of corporality, through the medium of the craft practices of the fiddler or harpist, into the breath of song as simultaneously enchantment and remembrance of loss. A figuring of the continual transformation inherent in the performed patterning of remembrance that – like the old ballads themselves - is a source of wonder and strange beauty, but also a contribution to an understanding of community that concludes with a finality in which only the wind and the rain remain.

The author would like to express his gratitude to Hayden Lorimer and John Wylie for allowing him sight of their forthcoming papers.

Yvonne Buchheim

Sound Water Beat

Public Performance
Cardigan Swimming Pool
Friday 23rd May 2008

It was an incredibly wet evening, there was one of those sudden downpours so people arrived literally dripping. I looked around to see who was there and there was a good cross-section of people, and far more people than the organisers had perhaps expected – it's a very unlikely venue for art. I got the feeling that some of the people were used to the building and probably came swimming there.

People were held outside for quite a while, which gave a theatrical dimension to the whole thing, and the pool had been made strange for that event, very successfully. The water was lit, there were people who were in bubbles, sitting on the water, big bubbles, you know those ones that you could walk on the water in.

And then the singing started – it was extraordinary. The singing played with the acoustic in the swimming pool in ways that you would like to play with it, you know, as a swimmer, you would like to get out and give it a bit of a belt because it's got that kind of acoustic but you probably never would.

There were two swimmers and they swam up and down, but they swam very differently so there was a kind of kinaesthetic component in that one of the swimmers swam in an irregular pattern and played with the water and the other one swam up and down very steadily for the whole period of time and the way of watching the swimmers was affected by the mood that was created by the music and the singing.

(Extract from an interview with an audience member)

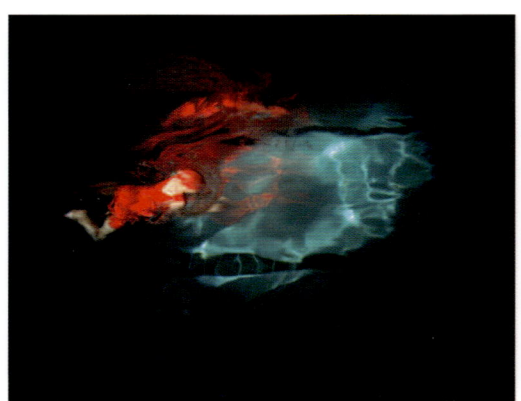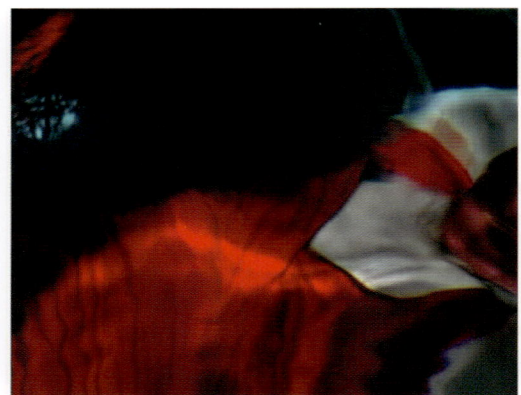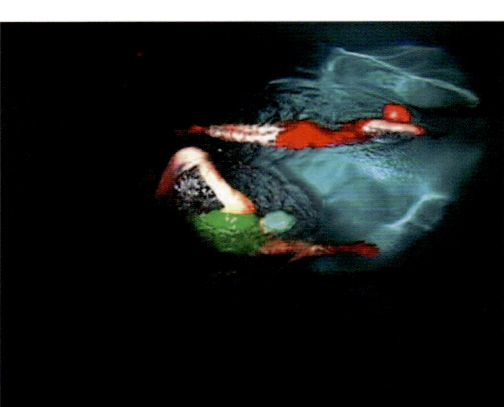

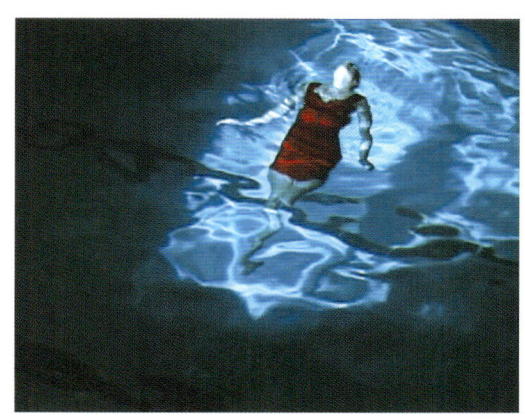 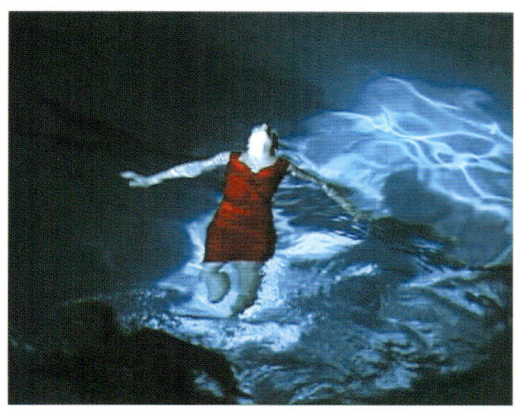 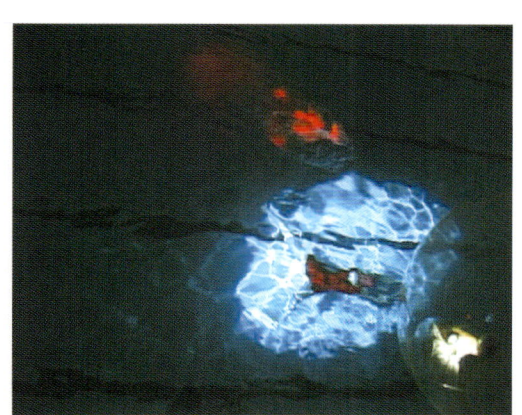

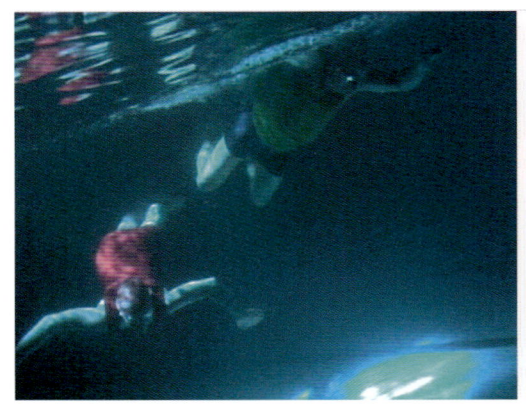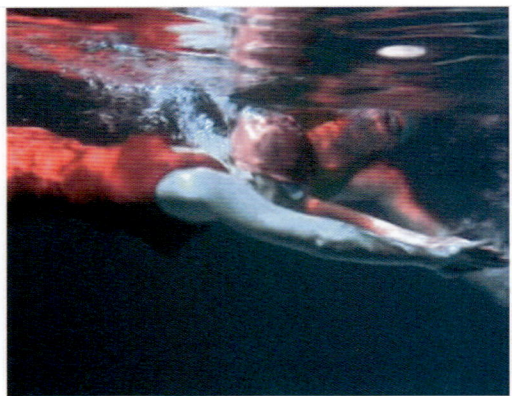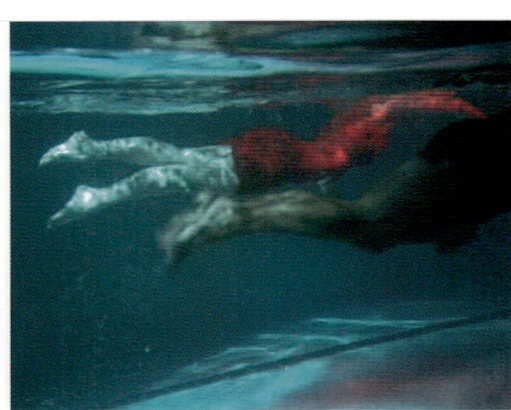

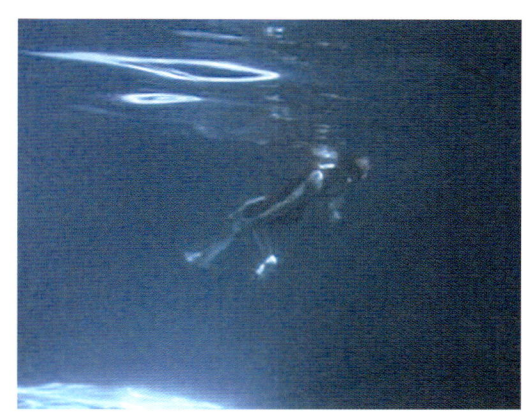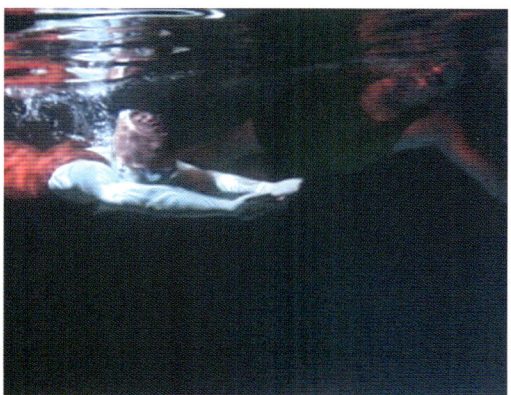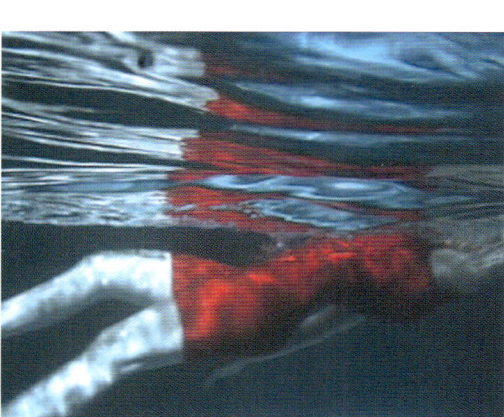

Yvonne Buchheim

Earworms

Sound Installation
Cardigan Swimming Pool
April–May 2009

'Civilization ends at the waterline.'
Hunter S. Thompson

'Take a music bath once or twice a week for a few seasons, and you will find that it is to the soul what the water bath is to the body.'
Oliver Wendell Holmes

Cardigan is closed to traffic when I arrive on a sleety afternoon in late April. A lone policeman languidly waves cars away, pointing them vaguely into the Ceredigion countryside. Nobody in this sleepy market town in West Wales seems to mind the delay and diversion; there is no road rage, or sense of urgency.

After the hold-up I've got less than an hour to make it to my destination: the local swimming baths, where I'm hoping to experience Yvonne Buchheim's underwater sound installation, *Earworms*. This draws on the artist's archive of over 800 informal recordings of people singing songs of their choice in Europe, the USA and Iran. I abandon the car, and set off on foot. The sleet has turned to sharp hail, and I'm getting very funny looks when I ask passers-by where the pool is.

A few wrong turns later, and I'm now running through the hail into the centre of town. Crowds line the streets, and nobody else has a rolled towel and swimming costume under their arm: they are here, I find out, for Barley Saturday, an annual parade of horses, vintage tractors and fancy agricultural vehicles. Stallions clip-clop by, bells and ribbons in their manes, and it turns out we are going the same way, as all the horse boxes are in the swimming pool car park. 'Follow the ponies' is the weirdest set of directions I've ever had for visiting an exhibition.

The pool, in an unprepossessing modern block, is almost empty thanks to the event outside and there are just three of us in the water. This gives me a near-private view of Buchheim's work – view

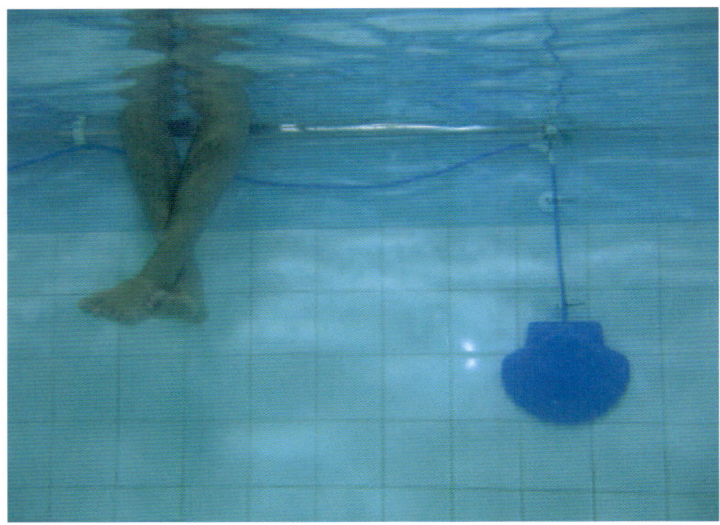

isn't quite the right term, though, as there's deliberately nothing to see in the pool area – detached from the usual atmosphere, noise and rituals of a busy swimming pool on a Saturday afternoon. But the peace and calm of the space, after such a boisterous and unlikely journey to get here, dramatically underlines the fact that swimming is about slipping into another realm. It's about temporarily shedding some, or all, of what you bring to the pool's edge as you enter the watery world of weightlessness and, in Buchheim's intervention, rich, imaginative possibility. Civilisation, as Hunter S. Thompson mooted, ends at the waterline. Or at least, it's put on hold.

One of the things I like most about *Earworms* is its playful, thoughtful oscillation between public space and private, personal or secret experience. This begins with the collection of songs. Buchheim asks individuals – on the street, in shops, in different countries and cultures, but always strangers in public – if she can record them singing a song. These are not performers, or professional singers, and the vast majority decline. Those that sing do so alone and unaccompanied, unaided too by karaoke lyrics on screen, just as they might when thinking themselves unheard in a quiet, or private, nook of daily life.

In the pool, it's the same creative juxtaposition of hidden and suddenly present. Apart from an easily missed information leaflet at the pool's reception, there is nothing to tell you that an artwork lurks unseen within the water. It's possible to swim entirely unaware of it if you don't venture underwater. Pool staff report that one swimmer thought she was hearing things; another heard the sounds but her friend swimming alongside didn't. I compare notes with the other swimmers after my visit and none of us recall the same songs. Like memory and dreams, which this installation reminds you of, the experience here is random, fluid, personal, fleeting and unreliable. Weeks later, I'm not sure if I heard a burst of a particular song ('I Never Promised You a Rose Garden'), or if I've heard it somewhere since and blurred the two together.

Buchheim is not alone in exploring the artistic potential of a public, liquid setting. Last month, Juliana Snapper presented an underwater opera, *You Who Will Emerge from the Flood*, at Manchester's defunct Victoria baths. Composer Michel Redolfi has staged over 150 underwater concerts since 1981, including *The Liquid City* at the Venice Biennale in 2006, aiming to immerse audiences, he says, in 'a bath of sound'. And last year's Lower Keys Underwater Music Festival in Florida was given a US presidential election theme, with Reefpublicans pitted against Democrabs. Thankfully, the Democrabs won.

The idea of a bath of sound, or as Oliver Wendell Holmes put it, a "music bath" comes close to the feeling of Buchheim's installation. It is a whole body experience; you can only hear it when immersed in water, and you are as you listen enveloped by the water carrying the sound. There are the obvious reasons why floating in water is soothing, with its echo of the womb, but Buchheim's use of the amateur singers gives her installation an edge over formal, polished spectacles staged underwater. There is something deeply affecting, listening to someone sing a favourite song alone, inevitably revealing something of themselves to us as they do – why else would so many dodge doing so? Buchheim embellishes this by deliberately leaving gaps between songs, and these offer a space of reflection (*What song would I choose? How would I sound? What was that last one called? My neck hurts in this position. How silly must I look?*) in the midst of what is an intense and charismatic individual journey through a secret, submerged sound archive.

Many of us ponder how to open up the experience of contemporary art to wider audiences, and to demystify the gallery for visitors without having to sideline rigorous, challenging artworks in the process. *Earworms* achieves all this, not least because to experience it is necessarily to engage with it as you float or swim. But it also underpins the uncomplicated physical pleasure of listening, suspended in water, with a strong undercurrent of ideas – ideas about where the bodily meets the imaginative; how performative it is to sing to a stranger, or listen to the results in a public pool; how an unseen, seemingly silent intervention alters the familiar, echoey soundscape of the municipal swimming baths; how perception is a collision of traces that seep away as fast as you can identify them.

The last song I hear, floating on my back, eyes closed, is *Que Sera Sera*, the anonymous singer a bit shaky on the verses but relieved and emboldened with each chorus. It's a fitting end to my experience of *Earworms*, with its celebration of the randomness of things ("whatever will be, will be") - the theme that quietly emerges from this barely-there public installation in west Wales one Barley Saturday.

Elizabeth Mahoney, 2009

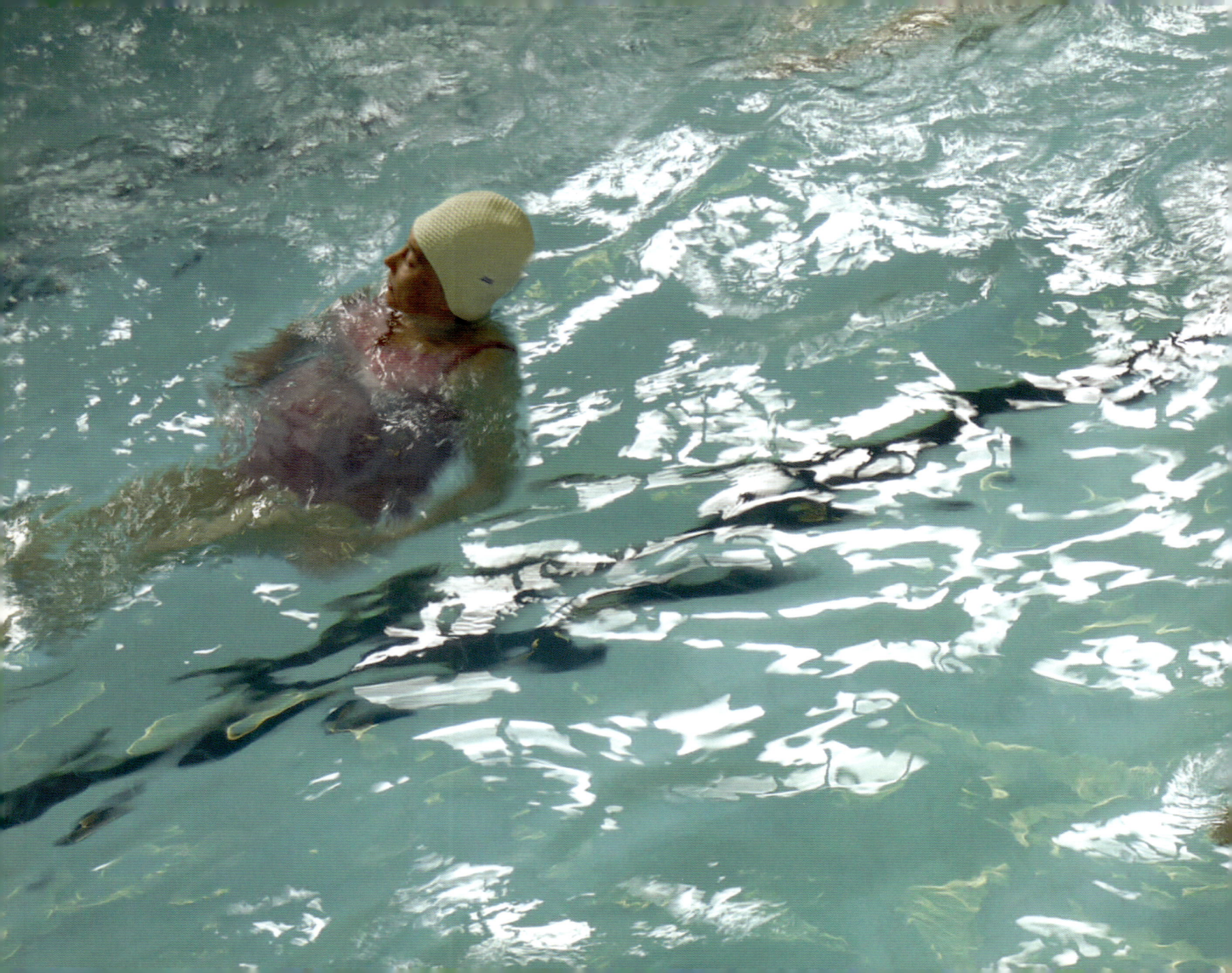

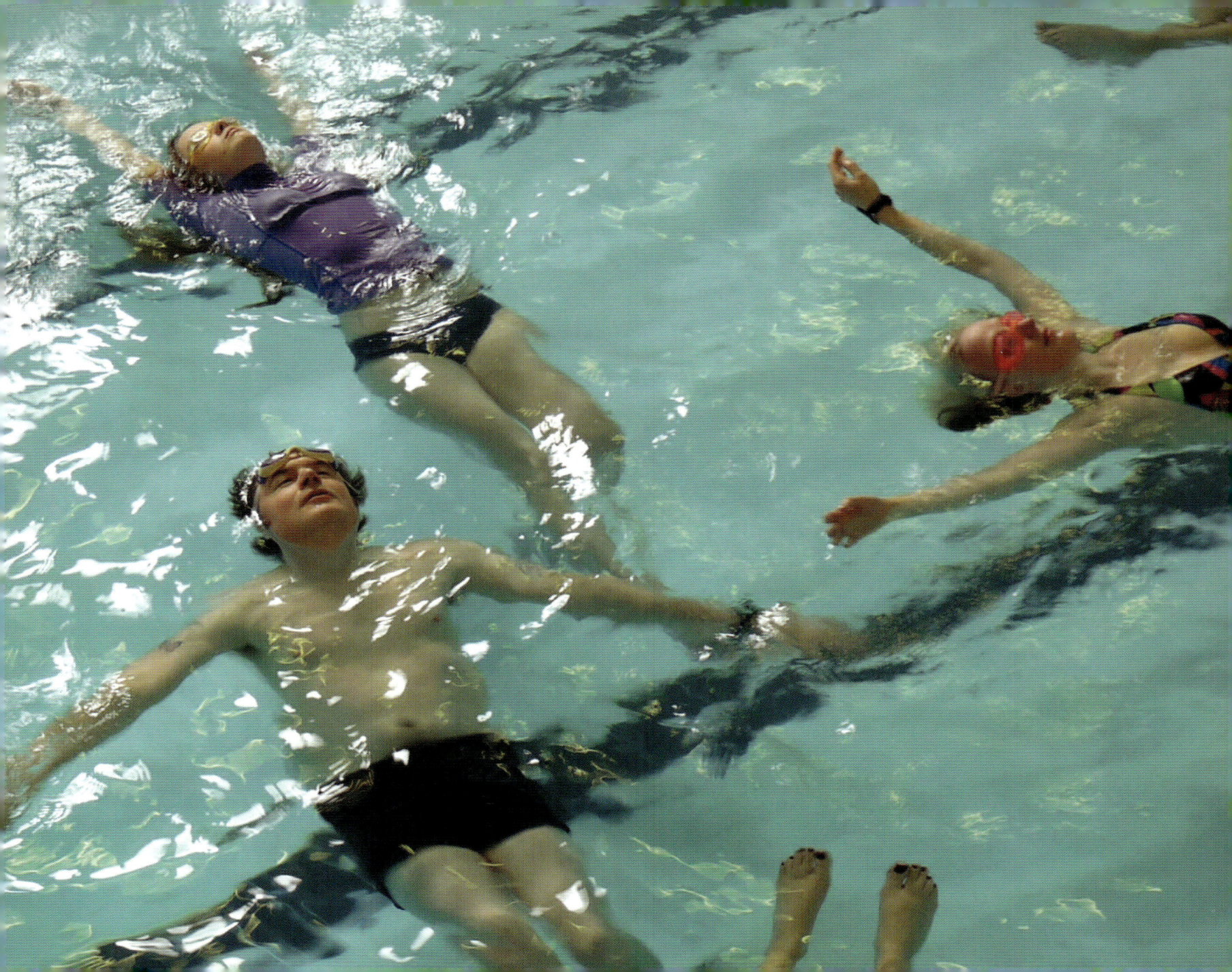

Notes on the Text

Introductory Essay by Ruth Jones: Experiments with Living Rituals/Arbrofi gyda Defodau Byw

1   Grimes, *Rite out of Place*, p. ix.
2   Kester, *Conversation Pieces*.

Bobby C. Alexander: Public Art in the Ritual Construction of Human Community

1   Turner, *Dramas, Fields, and Metaphors*.
2   Van Gennep, *Rites of Passage*.
3   See the references for Turner.
4   Turner cites Buber, *I and Thou*.
5   Bell, *Ritual Theory, Ritual Practice*.
6   Turner, *From Ritual to Theatre*.
7   See Schechner and Appel, *By Means of Performance*; Schechner, *Essays on Performance Theory*; Grimes, *Beginnings in Ritual Studies*; and Grimes, *Ritual Criticism*.
8   Turner, *From Ritual to Theatre*.
9   Compare Erving Goffman, *Frame Analysis*, on the dramaturgical model of human social interchange.
10 Turner, *From Ritual to Theatre*, p. 95.
11 For references to Grotowski in addition to those in the reference list, see Alexander, *Victor Turner Revisited*.
12 Turner, *From Ritual to Theatre*. On 'flow', see Csikszentmihalyi, *Beyond Boredom and Anxiety*.
13 Artaud, *The Theatre and Its Double*.
14 See, for example, Innes, *Holy Theatre*.
15 I would like to express my appreciation to William Henry Varner, a musician, composer, music educator, and my partner, for suggesting that I invite the audience for the Holy Hiatus symposium to create a ritual together.
16 Turner, *From Ritual to Theatre*, cites Schechner, *Ritual, Play, and Performance*.
17 I am indebted to Professor David A. Martin, a British sociologist of religion and dear friend, for the reference to Otto's *Idea of the Holy*. For a short discussion of Otto, see Ludwig, 'Rudolf Otto'. For an extended discussion of Otto's treatment of the holy, as well as the etymology of the word as distinct from the word sacred, see Oxtoby, 'Holy, Idea of The'.

Ruth Jones: Inventing Rituals – Inhabiting Places

1   Rothenbuhler, *Ritual Communication*, p. 6.
2   Schechner, *The Future of Ritual*, p. 228.
3   For a detailed analysis of definitions of ritual see Rothenbuhler, *Ritual Communication*, pp. 3–27.
4   Bloch, 'Symbols, song, dance and features of articulation', p. 38.
5   *Ibid.*
6   *Ibid.*
7   Tambiah rejects Bloch's distinction between ritual language (illocutionary) and ordinary day-to-day speech (prepositional), arguing that both styles may appear within a ritual, and in fact a fluid relationship exists between them.
8   Csordas, *Language, Charisma and Creativity*, p. 254.
9   Kreinath, *Ritual*.
10 Geertz in Kreinath, *Ritual*, p. 102.

11 *Ibid.*

12 Schechner, *The Future of Ritual*, p. 228.

13 *Ibid.*, p. 263.

14 Csordas, *Language, Charisma and Creativity*, p. 262.

15 Schechner, *The Future of Ritual*, p. 263.

16 See Alexander, *Victor Turner Revisted*, p. 23. Mary Douglas argues that the distinction between modern societies and 'primitive' ones is not that ritual is more prominent in the latter, but that primitive societies use ritual to create a self-contained and consistent universe, whereas modern societies use ritual to create subworlds that are not as tightly linked because modern societies are far less homogeneous.

17 Victor Turner in Alexander, *Victor Turner Revisted*, p. 35.

18 *Ibid.*, p. 18.

19 *Ibid.*, p. 36.

20 *Ibid.*

21 Schechner, *The Future of Ritual*, p. 20. Schechner draws on the work of Charles Laughlin and Eugene d'Aquili and colleagues. Ronald L. Grimes, *Rite out of Place*, pp. 138–40, scrutinizes these 'biogenetic' theories, and while he is sympathetic to the writers' perspective, he believes that their conclusions about the hardwiring of ritual activity in human consciousness is a generalised and unsubstantiated theory and does not take into account the fact that some cultures emphasise ritual much more than others and that ritual encompasses a huge range of activities. He suggests instead that certain kinds of ritual (predominantly trance and meditation) under certain circumstances can attune both sides of the brain in beneficial ways.

22 Schechner, *The Future of Ritual*, p. 233. See also pp. 240 and 256.

23 Ehrenreich, *Dancing in the Streets*, p. 23. Ehrenreich draws on research by Robin Dunbar, who suggests in his book *Grooming, Gossip, and the Evolution of Language* that the optimal palaeolithic group was about 150 people and that dance more than speech bonded these groups at an emotional level.

24 While the other four artworks were performative or event based, Anna Lucas's project differed in that its culmination was a video installation, and this created a different relationship with the audience. The installation offered an insight into the relationships that teenagers have with working animals in rural west Wales, and documented the rituals that accompany these interactions. Interviewees therefore saw it as 'about ritual' rather than creative of ritual. Caroline says that while she 'did not feel ritualised by it', the film presented 'the quiet looking at these different people doing their stuff, it was quite vulnerable. So I thought there was a kind of reverence, in looking into somebody's life in a kind of quiet way that was being brought out to you.'

25 Kester, *Conversation Pieces*, pp. 8–10.

26 Grimes, *Rite out of Place*, p. 146.

Iain Biggs: The Presence of Absence: Song, Ritual, and Place

1 Wylie, *Landscape, Absence and the Geographies of Love*.

2 Kearney, *Poetics of Imagining*.

3 For an overview of the fragmentation of a general sense of community in the UK since 1970 see http://news.bbc.co.uk/1/hi/uk/7759533.stm.

4 Kwon, *One Place after Another*, p. 156.

5 *Ibid.*, p. 164.

6 Lippard, *The Lure of the Local*, p. 196.

7   Frampton, quoted in Biggs, 'Educating "local cosmopolitans"', p. 19.

8   Stewart and Strathern, *Landscape, Memory and History*, p. 5.

9   Biggs, 'Educating "local cosmopolitans"', and 'Towards a polytheistic relationship to landscape'.

10   Casey, *Getting Back into Place*, p. 31.

11   Bennett, *The Enchantment of Modern Life*, p. 174.

12   Wylie, *Landscape, Absence and the Geographies of Love*, p. 6.

13   Biggs, *Between Carterhaugh and Tamshiel Rig*, and *Eight Lost Songs*.

14   Napier, *Masks, Transformation, and Paradox*, pp. 4–5.

15   Warner, *Fantastic Metamorphoses*, p. 2.

16   Bennett, *The Enchantment of Modern Life*, p.12.

17   Wylie, *Landscape, Absence and the Geographies of Love*.

18   Tuan, *Place, Art, and Self*, p. 44.

19   Solnit, *As Eve Said to the Serpent*.

20   Biggs *et al.*, 2007.

21   Wolff, *Resident Alien*, p. 32.

References

Alexander, Bobby C. (1991) *Victor Turner Revisted: Ritual as Social Change*. Atlanta, GA: Scholars Press.

Ardener, E. (1975) 'Belief and the problem of women'. In S. Ardener (ed.), *Perceiving Women*. London: Malaby Press.

Artaud, Antonin (1958) *The Theatre and Its Double*. Translated from the French by Mary Caroline Richards. New York: Grove Press.

Bell, Catherine (1992) *Ritual Theory, Ritual Practice*. Oxford: Oxford University Press.

Bennett, J. (2001) *The Enchantment of Modern Life*. Princeton, NJ: Princeton University Press.

Biggs, I. (2001) 'Educating "local cosmopolitans": the case for a critical regionalism in art education?' *Journal of Visual Art Practice*, 1(1), 16–24.

Biggs, I. (2004a) *Between Carterhaugh and Tamshiel Rig: A Borderline Episode*. Bristol: Wild Conversations Press for TRACE.

Biggs, I. (2004b) *Eight Lost Songs*. Isle of Wight: MakingSpace Publications.

Biggs, I. (2005) 'Towards a polytheistic relationship to landscape: issues for contemporary art'. *Landscape Research*, 30(1), 5–22.

Biggs, I., Abbassy, S., Millar, J. and Peters, G. (2007) *Debatable Lands Vol. 1*. Bristol: Wild Conversations Press (for TRACE).

Bloch, Maurice (1989) 'Symbols, song, dance and features of articulation: Is religion and extreme form of traditional authority?' in *Ritual, History and Power*. London and Atlantic Highlands, NJ: Athlone Press.

Buber, Martin (1970) *I and Thou*. Translated by Walter Kaufmann. New York: Charles Scribner's Sons.

Casey, E. (1993) *Getting Back into Place: Towards a Renewed Understanding of the Place-World*. Bloomington: Indiana University Press.

Casey, E. (2000) *Remembering: A Phenomenological Study*, 2nd edn. Bloomington: Indiana University Press.

Csikszentmihalyi, Mihaly (1975) *Beyond Boredom and Anxiety: The Experience of Play in Work and Games*. San Francisco: Jossey-Bass.

Csordas, T. J. (1997) *Language, Charisma and Creativity* (http://ark.cdlib.org/ark:/13030/ft2d5nb15g).

Dunbar, Robin (1996) *Grooming, Gossip, and the Evolution of Language*. Cambridge, MA: Harvard University Press.

Ehrenreich, Barbara (2007) *Dancing in the Streets: A History of Collective Joy*. London: Granta Books.

Goffman, Erving (1974) *Frame Analysis: An Essay on the Organization of Experience*. New York: Harper & Row.

Grimes, Ronald L. (1982) Beginnings in Ritual Studies. Lanham, MD: University Press of America.

Grimes, Ronald L. (1990) *Ritual Criticism: Case Studies in Its Practice, Essays on Its Theory*. Columbia: University of South Carolina Press.

Grimes, Ronald L. (2006) *Rite out of Place: Ritual, Media and the Arts*. Oxford and New York: Oxford University Press.

Grotowski, Jerzy (1968) *Towards a Poor Theatre*. New York: Simon and Schuster.

Grotowski, Jerzy (1977) 'In Search of Active Culture'. Public address, The Lindisfarne Institute, New York, 14 March.

Grotowski, Jerzy (1981) 'Vigil'. Public address at a benefit for

Jacek Zymslowski, Hunter College, The City University of New York, 20 May.

Grotowski, Jerzy (1982) Responses made in an open discussion in a class within the Theater Division of Columbia University, New York, 22 June 1982.

Haraway, D. J. (1991) *Simians, Cyborgs and Women: The Reinvention of Nature*. London: Free Association Books.

Heidegger, M. (1996) *Being and Time*. Albany: State University of New York Press.

Hurn, S. (2007) 'Cultural conditioning: constructions of equine obesity amongst Welsh Cob exhibitors'. *NES Journal of Equine Studies*, 2, 33–6.

Hurn, S. (2008a) 'What's love got to do with it? The interplay between sex and gender in the commercial breeding of Welsh Cobs'. Society and Animals, 16(1), 23–44.

Hurn, S. (2008b) 'The "Cardinauts" of the western coast of Wales: exchanging and exhibiting horses in the pursuit of fame'. *Journal of Material Culture*, 13(3), 335–55.

Ingold, T. (1994) 'From trust to domination: an alternative history of human–animal relations'. In A. Manning and J. Serpell (eds), *Animals and Human Society*. London: Routledge.

Ingold, T. (2000) *The Perception of the Environment*. London: Routledge.

Innes, Christopher (1981) *Holy Theatre: Ritual and the Avant Garde*. Cambridge: Cambridge University Press.

Jones, O. and Cloke, P. (2002) *Tree Cultures: The Place of Trees and Trees in Their Place*. Oxford: Berg.

Kearney, R. (1993) *Poetics of Imagining: From Husserl to Lyotard*. London and New York: Routledge.

Kester, Grant H. (2004) *Conversation Pieces: Community and Communication in Modern Art*. Berkeley, Los Angeles and London: University of Clifornia Press.

Kreinath, Jens (2005) *Ritual: Theoretical Issues in the Study of Religion* (http://www.pucsp.br/rever/rv4_2005/p_kreinath.pdf).

Kwon, M. (2002) *One Place after Another: Site-Specific Art and Locational Identity*. Cambridge, MA: MIT Press.

Lippard, L. (1997) *The Lure of the Local: Senses of Place in a Multicultural Society*. New York: The New Press.

Lorimer, H. (forthcoming) *Forces of Nature, Forms of Life: Calibrating Ethology and Phenomenology*.

Ludwig, Theodore M. (1987) 'Rudolf Otto'. In Mirces Eliade *et al.* (eds), *The Encyclopedia of Religion*, Vol. 11. New York: Macmillan.

Marvin, G. (2000) 'The problem of foxes: legitimate and illegitimate killing in the English countryside'. In J. Knight (ed.), *Natural Enemies: People–Wildlife Conflicts in Anthropological Perspective*. London: Routledge.

Massey, D. (2005) *For Space*. London: Sage.

Milton, K. (2005a) 'Anthropomorphism or egomorphism? The perception of nonhuman persons by human ones'. In J. Knight (ed.), *Animals in Person: Cultural Perspectives on Human–Animal Intimacies*. Oxford: Berg.

Mullin, M. (1999) 'Mirrors and windows: sociocultural studies of human–animal relationships'. *Annual Review of Anthropology*, 28, 201–24.

Mullin, M. (2002) 'Animals and anthropology'. *Society and Animals*, 10(4), 387–93.

Napier, A. (1986) *Masks, Transformation, and Paradox*. Berkeley: University of California Press.

Night Vigil (1979) Film of a performance of Grotowski's *Night Vigil* in Milan. Produced by the Atlas Theater Company.

Otto, Rudolf (1923). *The Idea of the Holy: An Inquiry into the Non-Rational Factor in the Idea of the Divine and Its Relation to the Rational.* Translated by John W. Harvey. (Originally published 1917; 2nd edition, London, New York: Oxford University Press, 1950; reprint, New York: Oxford University Press, 1970.)

Oxtoby, Willard G. (1987) 'Holy, Idea of The'. In Mirces Eliade *et al.* (eds), *The Encyclopedia of Religion,* Vol. 6. New York: Macmillan.

Rothenbuhler, Eric W. (1998) *Ritual Communication: From Everyday Conversation to Mediated Ceremony.* Thousand Oaks, CA, London and New Dehli: Sage.

Schechner, Richard (1977a) *Essays on Performance Theory: 1970–1976.* New York: Drama Book Specialists.

Schechner, Richard (1977b) *Ritual, Play, and Performance.* New York: The Seabury Press.

Schechner, Richard (1993) *The Future of Ritual: Writings on Culture and Performance.* London: Routledge.

Schechner, Richard and Appel, Willa (eds) (1990) *By Means of Performance: Intercultural Studies of Theatre and Ritual.* Cambridge: Cambridge University Press.

Solnit, R. (2001) *As Eve Said to the Serpent: On Landscape, Gender and Art.* Athens: University of Georgia Press.

Stewart, P. and Strathern, A. (eds) (2003) *Landscape, Memory and History: Anthropological Perspectives.* London: Pluto Press.

Tuan Y.-F. (2004) *Place, Art, and Self.* Santa Fe, NM: Center for American Places.

Turner, Victor (1969) *The Ritual Process: Structure and Anti-Structure.* Ithaca, NY: Cornell University Press.

Turner, Victor (1974) *Dramas, Fields, and Metaphors: Symbolic Action in Human Society.* Ithaca, NY: Cornell University Press.

Turner, Victor (1982) *From Ritual to Theatre: The Seriousness of Human Play.* New York: Performance Art Journal Publications.

Van Gennep, Arnold (1960) *The Rites of Passage.* Translated by Monika B. Vizedom and Gabrielle L. Caffee. Chicago: University of Chicago Press (originally published 1908).

Warner, M. (2002) *Fantastic Metamorphoses, Other Worlds.* Oxford: Oxford University Press.

Wolff, J. (1995) *Resident Alien: Feminist Cultural Criticism.* Cambridge: Polity Press.

Wylie, J. (forthcoming) *Landscape, Absence and the Geographies of Love.*

Image Credits

Page b. (left) *Drift* Simon Whitehead. (right) *Lure in Rule* Alastair MacLennan. Photographs by Ben Stammers 2008

Page 2. *Lure in Rule* Alastair MacLennan. Photograph by Ben Stammers 2008

Page 3. *Lure in Rule* Alastair MacLennan. Photograph by Noëlle Pollington 2008

Page 4-5. *Lure in Rule* Alastair MacLennan. Photograph by Ben Stammers 2008

Page 7. *Lure in Rule* Alastair MacLennan. Photograph by Noëlle Pollington 2008

Page 14?. Jerzy Grotowski 1983. Courtesy of Columbia University and Andy Harris. Photographer unknown.

Page 17. *Lure in Rule* Alastair MacLennan. Photograph by Noëlle Pollington 2008

Page 19. *Lure in Rule* Alastair MacLennan. Photograph by Kirsty Brooks 2008

Page 20. Audience response to *Lure in Rule* Alastair MacLennan. Photograph by Kirsty Brooks 2008

Pages 26 – 34. *Drift* Simon Whitehead. Photographs by Ben Stammers 2008

Page 41. *Drift* Simon Whitehead. Photograph by Noëlle Pollington 2008

Page 42. Audience response to *Untitled* Maura Hazelden. Photograph by Noëlle Pollington 2008

Page 43. *Sound Water Beat* Yvonne Buchheim. Stills from documentation 2008

Page 45. *Sound Water Beat* Yvonne Buchheim. Photograph by Noëlle Pollington 2008

Page 46. *Untitled* Maura Hazelden. Photograph by Noëlle Pollington 2008

Page 48. Audience response to *Drift* Simon Whitehead. Photograph by Noëlle Pollington 2008

Page 49. (top) *Lure in Rule* Alastair MacLennan. Photograph by Noëlle Pollington 2008

(bottom) *Drift* Simon Whitehead. Photograph by Kirsty Brooks 2008

Pages 54-59. *Untitled* Maura Hazelden. Photographs by Noëlle Pollington 2008.

Pages 60-61. *Untitled* Maura Hazelden. cctv stills by Jake Whittaker 2008

Page 64. *Paloma Ceffyl* Anna Lucas. Film stills 2005.

Page 68. *Begail Foxwell Whip* Anna Lucas. Installation view. Photograph by Kirsty Brooks 2008.

Page 71. *Little White Feather and the Hunter* Anna Lucas. Film stills 2008.

Page 72. Discussion between Anna Lucas and Samantha Hurn at *Holy Hiatus* symposium. Stills from documentation Ruth Jones.

Page 73. *Little White Feather and the Hunter* Anna Lucas. Film stills 2008.

Page 74. *Begail Foxwell Whip* Anna Lucas. Film still 2008

Pages 78 – 82. *Begail Foxwell Whip* Anna Lucas. Film stills 2008

Pages 93-96. Photographs by Iain Biggs 2007

Pages 100-103. *Sound Water Beat* Yvonne Buchheim. Stills from documentation 2008

Page 106. *Earworms* Yvonne Buchheim. Photograph by Ronnie Close 2008

Pages 108-109. *Earworms* Yvonne Buchheim. Photographs by Ruth Jones 2009

Biographies

Ruth Jones

Dr Ruth Jones is an artist and curator based in West Wales. She has exhibited widely in the UK, and internationally in Ireland, Poland, the USA, Spain and Canada. She studied Fine Art at Liverpool John Moores University and The University of Ulster, where she completed a masters degree in 1997 and a practice led DPhil in 2002. In 2006 she was awarded an AHRC Fellowship in Creative and Performing Arts at the University of the West of England, Bristol, exploring the relationships between ritual, place and community in lens-based and public art. Recent projects include *sleepers* (2006), a film and public art project in conjunction with Oriel Mwldan, Cardigan; *Vigil* (2008), a video installation about Strumble Head lighthouse; and *Cloddfa* (2010), a video installation exploring the disused quarries at Porthgain, Pembrokeshire.

Jones was a co-director of the Belfast based artist run gallery Catalyst Arts between 1997 and 1999. She also co-curated the exhibition *And the One Doesn't Stir without the Other* for the Ormeau Baths Gallery in 2003 and edited the accompanying publication. She has published articles in a number of catalogues and journals, including 'Betwixt and Between' in *no place I'm going to*, 'Becoming-hysterical, becoming-animal, becoming-woman in *The Horse Impressionists*', in *JVAP*, 3:2 and 'Between a flashing star and a gravestone, sleepers, liminality and communal dreaming' in the AHRC funded website *Imaginal Regions*.

www.ruthjonesart.co.uk

Bobby Alexander

Dr Bobby C. Alexander is Associate Professor of Sociology and Public Policy and Political Economy in the School of Economic, Political, and Policy Sciences at The University of Texas at Dallas. Dr Alexander received his PhD from Columbia University in Religious Studies; he was awarded a PhD in Systematic Theology by Union Theological Seminary. Dr Alexander is the author of two book monographs – originally published by the American Academy of Religion and currently in the catalogue of Oxford University Press. His publications in the fields of religious studies, social-scientific study of religion and ritual studies examine religion and social change.

Dr Alexander is co-author and co-editor of a forthcoming book based on a grant project funded by the US Department of Education's Fund for the Improvement of Post-Secondary Education, which he served as Project Director. His current research focuses on performance of credibility in the legal process of political asylum, and the contribution of religion and ritual to change in gender roles for immigrant women. His research has been funded by the Rockefeller Foundation, CrossCurrents: Association for Religion and Intellectual Life, Overbrook Foundation and American Academy of Religion. Dr Alexander serves on the Board of Directors of Yale University's Institute of Sacred Music.

Samantha Hurn

Dr Samantha Hurn is lecturer in Social Anthropology at the University of Wales, Lampeter. She specializes in anthrozoology or the comparative study of human interactions with non-human animals in a wide range of cultural contexts. Her research interests include the different ways in which humans and non-human animals perceive and engage with their environments and each other, and the various forms of indirect, inter-species communication which occur during these interactions with particular reference to farming, hunting and outdoor leisure pursuits (e.g. horse riding). She is also concerned with investigating the ways in which animals are selectively bred in response to specific environmental conditions, or human aesthetic ideals and functional expectations of how an animal should 'perform'.

Dr Hurn's current research focuses on cross-cultural human relationships with 'charismatic mega fauna', notably big cats, wolves and primates. She is considering the ways in which practical engagements with these animals, which are frequently 'problematic' in the eyes of the humans who have to share the same environments, have informed local cultural understandings and resulted in complex mythological representations. These mythologies have implications in terms of conservation, and Hurn is interested in investigating local ideas about predatory or transgressive species with a view to assisting conservation efforts.

Iain Biggs

Dr Iain Biggs is Reader in Visual Art Practice in the Faculty of Creative Arts, University of the West of England, Bristol; Director of the Place, Location, Context and Environment Research Centre (PLaCe); and a co-convener of the national network LAND[2]. He acts as Director of Supervised Research for the Faculty of Creative Arts and is a specialist in arts practice-led research. Iain trained as a painter and printmaker at the University of Leeds and undertook an MA by thesis at the Royal College of Art, but describes his current practice as an ethnographically inflected variant of 'deep mapping'.

Dr Biggs is currently finishing the second of a three-part collaborative expanded bookwork project – *Debatable Lands* – which involves collaboration with other artists, a musician and academics from a wide range of disciplines in the humanities and social sciences. The project uses traditional Borders ballads as a starting point for animating a rich interdisciplinary 'conversation' around questions of identity, place, politics, belief and belonging. He is also currently the principal investigator for a collaborative interdisciplinary ESRC-funded arts-led project in rural north Cornwall that will 'deep map' the relationship between older people and their landscape/environment.

Alastair MacLennan

Alastair MacLennan is based in Belfast and was a critical figure in the development of experimental performative practices during the 1970s and 1980s in Northern Ireland. He was a founding member of the international research group ARE (Art, Research, Exchange) and he joined the European performance art group Black Market International in 1989. In 1985, he established a masters course at the University of Ulster and between 1992 and 2008 he was Professor of Fine Art. Alastair has exhibited widely in Europe, North and South America and Asia and represented Ireland at the Venice Bienniale in 1997. The Ormeau Baths Gallery presented a major retrospective and publication, *Knot Naught*, in 2003. He has received numerous awards including the 'Lifetime Achievement Award' from Trace, Cardiff Art in Time in 2007. MacLennan's 'actuations' – which he describes as a direct realisation of actuality – open up a space where the gap between the performer and the viewer is reduced or even annulled by drawing the audience into a different state through meditative and ritual activity that can be profoundly moving.

www.vads.ac.uk/collections/maclennan

Simon Whitehead

Movement artist Simon Whitehead works from his base in rural West Wales. Originally trained as a geographer and dancer, over the last 15 years he has developed a body of work from pedestrian practices; made at walking pace his works are place-sensitive and involve a process of ritual reconstruction through the body, live performance, dance, sound and film. Whitehead was a recipient of a Creative Wales Award in 2005 from the Arts Council of Wales. He was Visiting Artist at the Yorkshire Sculpture Park 2005–6, where he developed *Walks to Illuminate*, a series of nocturnal walks for the public. In 2009 he completed *Scatter* (pedestrian-borne seed) in central London, he made *Run Like a Horse* as part of a residency in Laboral, Spain, and collaborated on the residency FIELDWORK with dance artist Jennifer Monson in New York City. Over the last 12 years he has collaborated closely with Melbourne-based sound artist Barnaby Oliver. They are currently working on a new project, PINGS, exploring the geographical space between them through rivers, sound and performance (www.untitledstates.net). Simon is a founder member of *ointment*, an itinerant artists collective, and in 2006 he published an anthology of his work, *Walking to Work*.

Maura Hazelden

Maura Hazelden is a multi-disciplinary artist working from West Wales. Originally trained in dance, she has since studied surface pattern and illustration, multi-disciplinary computer application and fine art: performance and photovisual, Cardiff (UWIC). She also taught fashion and textiles contextual studies at West Wales School of the Arts. Maura has been part of the *ointment* collective of artists since their inception in 2001, creating performances and installations including at Forest Art Festival, Darmstadt, with Simon Whitehead and residencies in West Wales and Quebec, Canada, with Boreal Art/Nature. Her exhibitions/performances include showings in Cardiff at: g39, Tactile Bosch, Oriel Canfas, Cardiff Art in Time 1999 and 2007; as well as Aberystwyth Museum; Bandits Images: Festival of Audio Visual & Multimedia Art, France; Osnabrük Media Arts Festival, Germany; Oriel Mwldan and with Diversions Dance Company.

The six hour *Holy Hiatus* performance, investigating repetition and prayer with sonic artist Lou Laurens, is building into a layered yearly event. Hazelden's work wanders through the domestic, memory and perception, the land; seeking the sensual; investigating the subliminal, the liminal. From order to evanescence: solid to vapour: experience to memory. The outcomes take various forms: performance/action/live art; photovisual and installation – sometimes all together. Currently she is moving into using writing within the fine art performance context.

www.maurahazelden.blogspot.com

Anna Lucas

Anna Lucas makes moving image work that develops observations of social networks and specific institutions or spaces. The works often focus on the intersection between the manmade and natural environment. Frequently the films portray people whose specific knowledge and devotion to what they do provides them with faith in, or escape from, the quotidian. Her recent major commission *Little White Feather and the Hunter* is a single screen video and accompanying book loosely re-telling the story of Native American Princess Pocahontas, touring in the UK and USA. Her films collectively named *Here and Your Here*, shown at FACT, Liverpool (2007) and Konstcentrum, Gavle, Sweden (2009), are based on complex themes connected to unusual plants found in Brixton markets, South London, Peru and the Middle East. 16mm films *Seventh Heaven* (2006) and *Begail Foxwell Whip* (2008) explore the diverse experience of teenagers at school in East London and working with animals in rural Wales respectively. Her latest 16mm film *Demonstration 50.15* and a series of 'blind movie' drawings come from a period of research in the anatomy lab whilst on a Wellcome Trust Fellowship at Deptartment of Physiology, Anatomy and Genetics and Ruskin School of Fine Art and Drawing at Oxford University.

Yvonne Buchheim

Yvonne Buchheim was born in Weimar and lives in Bristol where she is a Senior Lecturer at the University of the West of England. Her ongoing Song Archive Project functions as a framework to question cultural belief values and playfully suggests complex identities through song. Her art practice explores contemporary song culture in a variety of media, ranging from video to site-specific installation, performance and live art.

Buchheim has been awarded artist residencies and commissions in the UK, Ireland, France, Germany, the USA and Iran. Recent solo exhibitions include the Cheekwood Museum of the Art, Nashville, USA (2008); Butler Gallery, Ireland (2007) and Oriel Davies Gallery, Wales (2007). Recent group exhibitions include the Wallace Gallery, New York, USA, North+South commissions at the Southampton City Art Gallery (2007) and EV+A, Limerick (2006). She was awarded the Good Ideas Award from SAFLE, Wales (2007), resulting in two works for *Holy Hiatus:* a public performance *Sound Water Beat* (2008) and an underwater sound installation *Earworms* (2009), both at the Cardigan Swimming Pool in West Wales.

www.song-archive.org

Acknowledgements

Ruth Jones would like to thank Theatr Mwldan for their support of the project and assistance with publicity, Bill and Ann Hamblett at The Small World Theatre for accommodating the *Holy Hiatus* Symposium, Reuben Knutson for help with marketing and technical support, Sean Dowdall for his support and assistance with installing the works, Sarah Pace for carrying out and transcribing the interviews with audience members and Iain Biggs for his unwavering encouragement over the years.

Yvonne Buchheim would like to thank Ruth Jones, Ronnie Close, Lloyd Davies and the Cardigan Swimming Pool staff, Cinzia Mutigli and Safle, Maggie Nicols, Paul Uden, Hedz Llewelyn, Ian Davies, Michelle Harris, Amber Bolwell, Matt White, Anna Lucas, Sean Dowdall, Robert Lowe, Ffion Ann Delve, Cerys Price, Serena Williams, Mike Shoring, John Turner, Wyn and Fflach.

Anna Lucas would like to thank Ioan Jones, Holly Foxwell and James Jeavons for participating in the filming of *Begail Foxwell Whip*.

Maura Hazelden would like to thank Jacob Whittaker for technical support and documentation.

Art and Photography Books from Parthian

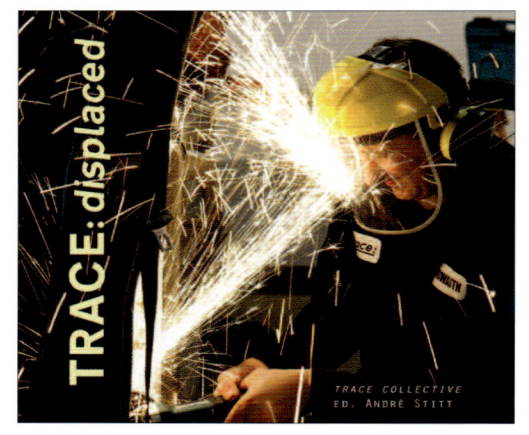

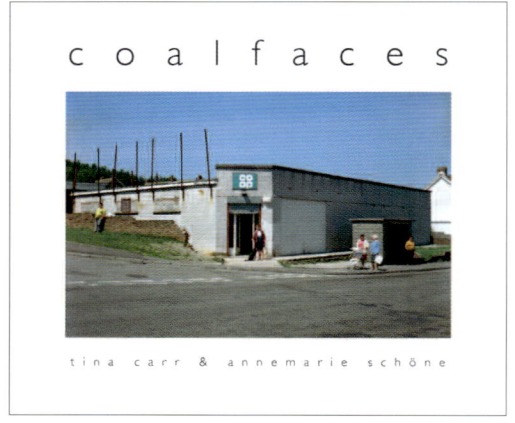

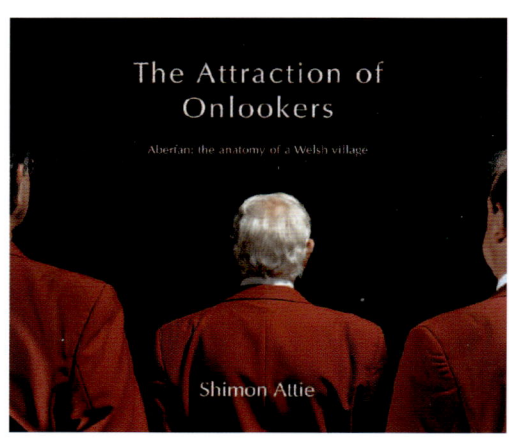

www.parthianbooks.com